護照

新外字第捌號

湖南省政府　　為

發給遊歷護照事據湖南私立雅禮中學校勞校長

啟祥呈稱本校美籍英文教員高德華現年二十三歲乘

暑假之便擬往雲南廣西等處遊歷呈請發給護照前来合

行發給合亟二護照...軍民長官及地方關卡查驗

Teaching in Wartime China

Edward V. Gulick

Teaching in Wartime China

A Photo-Memoir, 1937–1939

Edward V. Gulick

The University of Massachusetts Press   *Amherst*

Copyright © 1995 by
The University of Massachusetts Press
All rights reserved
Printed in the United States of America
ISBN 0-87023-912-0
LC 93-21344
Designed by Milenda Nan Ok Lee
Set in Sabon by Keystone Typesetting, Inc.
Printed and bound by Thomson-Shore, Inc.

Library of Congress Cataloging-in-Publication Data
Gulick, Edward Vose.
    Teaching in wartime China : a photo-memoir, 1937–1939 /
by Edward V. Gulick.
        p.   cm.
    ISBN 0-87023-912-0 (alk. paper)
    1. Gulick, Edward Vose — Journeys — China.
2. Author, American — 20 century — Biography.
3. Sino-Japanese Conflict, 1937–1945.   I. Title.
PS3557.U44T43   1994
420'.71'151 — dc20
[B]   93-21344
                            CIP

British Library Cataloguing in Publication data are available.

Publication of this book has been made possible by a generous
grant from the Chiang Ching-Kuo Foundation for International
Scholarly Exchange (USA), Washington, D.C.

For Betty with admiration and much love

Acknowledgments and Thanks

My profound thanks to the many gifted and generous individuals who have helped in a variety of ways — in reading, and reacting to, the emerging MS; in handling finances, in verifying data, suggesting improvements, and editing both text and pictures:

Paul Cohen   Elizabeth Lieberman
Fred Drake   Shirley Quinn
Mark Edwards   Burton Rogers
Frank Hutchins   Karin Rosenthal
Frank Hutchins, Jr.   Sophie Sa
Hwang Chien-hou   Peter Stead
Elsie Landstrom   Bruce Wilcox

Special thanks to the Chiang Ching-Kuo Foundation, whose subsidy grant made publication possible.

Contents

Maps

Foreword

This is a fascinating and deeply compelling memoir of a young American's experience teaching in a boys' school in Hunan province, China, in the late 1930s. Its author, Edward Gulick, who later went on to become an admired diplomatic historian and biographer and taught for many years in the history department at Wellesley College,[1] details in highly personal language his responses, intellectual and emotional, to the riveting events of the day. Since the main contemporary development was the outbreak of the Sino-Japanese segment of World War II, which impinged on Gulick and his school in the most direct and disruptive way, the memoir provides a uniquely localized record of China's wartime experiences. Although we often hear of the long overland trek from the eastern part of the country to the southwest made by Chinese institutions of higher learning in the early stages of the war, no other account that I know of focuses on the experiences of a secondary school right in the heart of an area where the Japanese were actively engaged.

But the war, for all of its importance, isn't the lone focal point of Gulick's memoir. We also get a close-up portrait of the operations of a boys' secondary school established and shaped by Americans (it was part of the Yale-in-China program), as part of a particular kind of Christian missionary activity in China

[1] Gulick's principal publications are *Europe's Classical Balance of Power: A Case History of the Theory and Practice of One of the Great Concepts of European Statecraft* (Ithaca: Cornell University Press, 1955 [reprinted by Norton in 1967]) and *Peter Parker and the Opening of China* (Cambridge, Mass.: Harvard University Press, 1973).

during those years. The book that Gulick's account reminds me of most is Ruth Hemenway's *A Memoir of Revolutionary China, 1924–1941*,[2] which also dealt in intimate terms with the experiences of an American "good samaritan" in China. Hemenway was a woman, a physician, and a good deal more agnostic in her Christianity than Gulick. Nevertheless, her account, like his, recorded the efforts of one caring American to do something of benefit for other human beings. Also like Gulick, Hemenway, too, was immensely interested in and sympathetic to all that was going on around her in her Chinese environment and opened for the reader a window on her private feelings and reactions and personal growth over time. One other way, rather more unusual, in which the two memoirs are strikingly similar is in the strongly visual emphasis of both. Hemenway's book included a wonderful selection of watercolors that the author painted, depicting in a naïve style what she had seen and experienced in China, while Gulick's account really is, as its title proclaims, a *photo* memoir.

And the photographs are superb. They are remarkably good technically, considering the equipment Gulick had to work with. They are full of human interest. They supply a luxuriant record of scenes, events, and individuals referred to in the prose narrative and do so in a far more integrated way than is customarily the case. What Gulick offers us, in other words, is not a written memoir occasionally highlighted by photographic material, but rather a truly "dual-media" record of his experience, the photographs and the prose informing and enriching each other at every step along the way.

This book will be of interest to students of Chinese history who want to know what it was like "on the ground" to cope with the excitement, terrors, and tragedy of the Sino-Japanese War. It will appeal to that part of the public that is especially sympathetic to Christian missionary and/or humanitarian endeavor. Most of all, the book is sure to be appreciated and enjoyed by people who simply like to look at very good pictures.

Paul A. Cohen
Wellesley College
March 1993

[2] Hemenway's book, edited and introduced by Fred W. Drake, was published by the University of Massachusetts Press in 1977.

Introduction

     This is the account of my involvement with a Chinese school at a critical moment in its, and world, history. Confronted with possible invasion and military occupation, the school leadership decided to move the school from a provincial capital to refugee quarters in a remote and obscure river town. It is an account of how both faculty and students rose to the challenge of that move away from home, from city to countryside, from peacetime to wartime, from affluence to poverty, and somehow turned potential disaster into a triumphant year of education. This account is also about international relations, but in a very special way — less as the acts of foreign offices, and more as the bicultural contacts of unremarkable and caring human beings.

     The locale was Hunan province, a subtropical part of the interior of China. The school was the Yali Union Middle School, a prominent boarding school for Chinese boys, ages 13 to 18. The period was 1937–39, the opening years of a great war between China and Japan that led not only to a deep penetration of the Chinese mainland by Japanese invaders but to multiple catastrophes and revolutionary change for both powers.

     There are so many extravagant and conflicting stories about missionaries that I want to show a slice of an enlightened mission enterprise in Central China, revealing aspects of the late phase of mission history and its role in the modernization of a traditional society. More specifically, I want to give the feel of daily events in 1937–39 within one notable mission school, telling the stories of individuals, both American and Chinese, who were engaged in a remarkable, bicultural educational effort, in which the Chinese and Americans of today can take great pride. And I want to celebrate the heroic response of ordinary people to the tumult and trauma of the devastating Japanese invasion of Central China in those years.

One of the many remarkable aspects of the pre-Communist Yale-in-China enterprise is that it can serve as a prototype for virtually any amount of future work with Third World countries. It met genuine needs. It avoided being unpleasantly intrusive. It was modest, effective, good-spirited, and inexpensive. It deserves to be more widely known in a world that increasingly needs helping hands which are neither government inspired nor government directed, but sensitively and lovingly run by well-organized civilians. Its conception was sound, with its reliance on a genuine working together, with an American jump-start for schools and medical establishments, and then with a systematic handing over of the leadership and operation to the Chinese.

Because much of that history is now forgotten, I need to position the educational microcosm of our school within the larger, historical context of Sino-Japanese and world events in the 1930s. And, since being there was one of the most vivid experiences of my life, I want to relate it all to my personal development as a participant and sympathetic observer. Thus, this account is unavoidably an unstable mixture of the personal, the institutional, and the international, of the minuscule and the immense.

. . .

My connection with China and Yali (pronounced yah-lee) began during senior year at Yale when I was hired by the Yale-in-China organization to teach English for two years in China. Yale-in-China sponsored a cluster of educational and medical institutions, of which Yali was one. They had been established in the capital of Hunan province by a group of young Yale graduates early in the twentieth century. The founders had been eager to demonstrate Christian fellowship by serving as educators and doctors in Hunan during a period when the antique Manchu government of China was awash in a sea of problems. Yale-in-China (today Yale-China) had a home office in New Haven to raise funds in support of its institutions in China and to recruit American personnel, chiefly for the Yali English Department.

In 1937, the year I graduated from Yale, China seemed only a distant abstraction. For my college generation reality was more persuasively represented by the recent Great Depression, the New Deal, the Roosevelts, and the lunar bleakness of Europe's international relations. For those of us who were interested in international affairs, the European state-system was inevitably the center of our attention, because in that era Europe ran most of the world. Britain, France, Russia, Portugal, Italy, Belgium, and the Netherlands—each controlled a vast empire. That alone made Europe crucial in world importance, but it also meant that disorder within Europe could destabilize the very structure of the global system as it then existed.

Those special circumstances gave Europe's international relations in the 1930s a peculiar intensity and complexity, now half-forgotten by a generation beset by its own gigantic, but different, problems. Malign leadership guaranteed that there was a major crisis virtually every week, and often two or more parallel crises—something that the European mechanisms of international statecraft were never well-equipped to handle.

China, on the other hand, was not only distant, disorganized, and weak, but it appeared so inconsequential that it had not yet entered American political calculations. Virtually no western universities in the 1930s offered substantial work in Chinese history, politics, economics, or language. Almost no American intellectuals understood either how important China had been historically or how atypical and deceptive her current weakness was. Thus, my photo-memoir of work in central China a long generation ago is in part an account of the discovery by one individual of a truth that his society did not then acknowledge—that China had a history and a culture and a future that could affect us all.

· · ·

Aged twenty-two in 1937, I was very much a product of the inter-war years—an idealist interested in social justice, a Christian pacifist with a strong commitment to the study of international relations, a New England Yankee by adoption and education, an individual with a Congregationalist's conscience about the importance of work, and a paralytic

3

inability to spend money joyfully. I was a regular attender of Sunday services at Battell Chapel to hear the superb choir and those remarkable guest preachers who did so much to shape the moral outlook of a whole generation. They taught me to be more interested in Christian simplicities and in making action fit profession, than in religious speculation or theological niceties. Yet, I was most at home in the classroom or reading; next came playing squash, watching varsity athletics or making my Saturday evening pilgrimage to one of the local movie houses, where a new Marx Brothers film often served to erase the week's discomforts and disappointments.

Notwithstanding its social snobberies, Yale was very well organized for someone without money, so I could manage an education there by a combination of scholarships, waiting on tables, bursary jobs, and summer savings. My mother, believing devoutly in college education, contributed what her teacher's salary permitted. I was deeply absorbed in my education and so busy that I hardly had time to develop solid habits, much less cultivate vices.

I emerged from all of this as an individual valuing scholarship and humor, putting decency ahead of dialectics, and tending to overvalue poise and the stiff upper lip. Independent to the point of being rather isolated, I was not practised in showing or receiving affection, although I was quick to respond to warmheartedness. As a generation we all had our uncertainties; my own diffuse insecurity involved much self-doubt, a sometimes crippling shyness, a vague sense of guilt, and a residual stammer which was none the less painful for being generally well hidden. All these were wrapped up in a good deal of kidding and laughter and academic enthusiasms. Whatever the mix of skills and shortcomings, I felt reasonably sure that I wanted to go into teaching, and that I wanted to combine a hiatus in my formal education with a job overseas.

These, then, were aspects of the individual in his twenty-third year who was about to undertake what today is just a tiring plane ride, but what in 1937 seemed more like trying to get to the other side of the moon.

. . .

In the account which I am presenting my memories are buttressed by more than a thousand black-and-white photographs which I took in

1937–39, and some of which are reproduced here. They were taken with what would now be regarded as trivial, not to say hopeless, equipment. I had bought in Germany on my way out to China a Wirgin camera which had a 3.5 Meyer Görlitz lens and was roughly the 35 mm equivalent of Eastman's Brownie. Small, light, and unadorned, it had the one lens and one cloud filter. For gauging light, I relied on guesswork and God's mercy, assisted by a little tube that, when held up to the subject, admitted light in graded grays, one of which could be translated into a combination of f-stop setting and shutter speed.

Because film was not readily available in interior China, I bought in a Hong Kong photo shop a round tin containing one hundred feet of movie film and was given a hatful of empty casettes. Using the hospital darkroom in Changsha, I cut the movie film and filled the casettes with sections of it. It was Eastman black-and-white panatomic on a nitrate base, a good staple of that period.

Since the subtropical climate of Hunan was rich in molds, I kept the film in various tins, usually taped shut. After exposure, I developed the film myself or sometimes had it done, and then put the negatives back into tins, where they remained without my seeing positives, as a rule, until months later. In retrospect, I am impressed by my young man's doggedness in the face of time-consuming obstacles when I was busy with a lot of other things.

In addition to the pictures, my work is supported by information from friends who shared my years in Hunan, by my letters home, which were carefully saved, and by relatively elaborate journals which I usually wrote up each weekend during those two years in China. In going over this material, I have also been impressed by the remarkable access we had. There were no political cosmetics between China and us—no guides, no prophylactic partitions, no stage-managed tours. With nothing organized for us, we earned laboriously what we found out. Our contacts had their limitations, but the Americans at Yali were genuinely in touch with the daily lives of many Chinese—students, parents, teachers, servants, shopkeepers, boatmen, housewives, restauranteurs, ricksha boys, gatemen, nurses, doctors, hospital technicians, businessmen, officials, returned students—a wide selection from the local scene.

My material has reminded me of what incredible juxtapositions one's journals include. The entry for one week, chosen at random from my second year, touched on baseball, romance, an encounter with dogs, acute physical ailments, the overflight of eighteen Japanese planes, the comings and goings of colleagues, the offer of the presidency of Berea College to our boss, Frank Hutchins, and his refusal (he later was persuaded to accept), and finally the activities of our neighbors' nanny goat to whom twin kids were being born on the path in front of their house. The mother walked about, unconcernedly browsing, with the emergent head sticking out of her posterior, while the first kid attempted to nurse. And I even wrote down our chaplain's observation that this scene illustrated our multiple life processes.

In the present account I will inevitably speak with two voices — one, the voice of the young man who was so moved by the exposure to China in the late 1930s; the other, that of the historian who pondered the experience at some length in the course of teaching the history of modern China and Japan for a dozen years to Wellesley College students. I have tried to make it clear which voice is speaking, so that the young man isn't given wisdom and insights beyond his years.

.   .   .

It now seems to me that World War II more than anything else shaped our world in the third quarter of the twentieth century. If that is so, it is of consequence to understand the omissions and commissions of the 1930s which led to that war. My instincts as a professional historian encourage me to try to preserve the memory and understanding of the unique nature and special pressures of the 1930s, among them the educational atmosphere of China before the conformities of the Maoist revolution.

In that sense, this book — which is focussed on a young man and a remote school — is about international affairs.

.   .   .

A word about spelling: generally I have used Wade-Giles romanization, but with exceptions found in the Postal Atlas of China, or our own variants when they correspond to our regular usage, such as, Yo-lo Shan, Soochow, Hangchow, Sun Yat Sen.

Arrival in China

      I reached Hong Kong with my classmate, John Runnalls—both of us heading for Yale-in-China—after three taxing weeks on the *Conte Bianco Mano*, a grand Italian liner designed for the cold weather of the North Atlantic and recently placed without appropriate alterations on the tropical run between Italy and Hong Kong. After stifling for the duration of that long voyage we woke at dawn on Sunday, September 12, 1937, for our approach to Kowloon with the star-sown hillside of Hong Kong to portside.

      Arrival was chaotic, but in our travelers' uncertainties over hotel, baggage, currency, and transportation to the interior of China, we discovered to our infinite relief the welcoming face of a friend from Yale, Rocky Chin, last seen by us in New Haven four months earlier and now a recent arrival from Vancouver. He was planning, like us, to go into the interior. I had left our luggage under the care of a baggage man without asking for a receipt. Expecting to find him at customs, I was vastly disconcerted when there proved to be no customs. We were then condemned to hours of casting about at docks, warehouses, railroad station, and consulate before rounding up our items. We had to locate yet another warehouse containing other baggage which had come by ship across the Pacific. Still without a place to sleep, we were invited by Rocky's uncle to use overnight a room, below his own apartment, where a wedding reception was to be held two days hence. But the invitation had to be withdrawn when neighbors protested that it risked bad luck for the marriage. We found other accommodations and then ate in a Western restaurant to bid a ritual farewell, as we mistakenly thought, to Western cooking for most of the next two years, the duration of our contracts with Yale-in-China.

Then, pitched headlong as we were into a new cultural universe, we spent much of the afternoon, evening, and next day simply staring in fascination, looking at shops and people, watching a man in the market expertly clean and filet fish, seeing how meat purchases were carried with neat loops of straw, how street hairdressers topdressed coiffures with a mysterious substance, thick and shiny. We watched the comings and goings at the waterfront, coolies endlessly carrying, women moving startlingly large loads of fruit and goods, junks loaded with crates of chickens, little children running about naked, and funerals noisily in progress. We watched the incredible swarm of marine activity both harborside and in the sheltered deep water between Kowloon and Hong Kong Island. Back and forth on the ferry we went, each time struck by the beauty of it all; up the funicular for the great vista from the Peak over deepwater port, islands, peninsula, and the high hills of the Republic of China in the haze to the north.

Hong Kong seemed more entrepôt than cultural center. Its fascination lay in its matchless mixtures of East and West and its magnificent setting. The view at night from Kowloon was like looking at the lights of Manhattan from Brooklyn Heights—with a mountain thrown in for a bit of grandeur. Hong Kong's heat and humidity, however, eased for me the pain of departure.

Up at dawn on the fourteenth, we ferried to Kowloon, getting to the station in time to find it bursting full of people waiting for the 8:33, our train to Canton. John stood over our baggage while I attempted to collect my trans-Pacific freight at the Dollar Line warehouse with the assistance of an American lady who was waiting for a bus and who could speak Cantonese to the coolies in the warehouse. She seized the occasion to speak to me about living in the Center of the Will of God. "If you don't know what that is, it is time you began to find out." The coolies told her the warehouse would not open until nine, postponing our departure

8

until the 12:50. I spent the morning searching the piers in a fine rain, and clambering over jumbled warehouse freight, and was finally rewarded by finding trunk and boxes.

Our first-class seats to Canton gave us ample room, an endless supply of tea, and clouds of cinders. As the train mounted the peninsula, we gazed at faces in the railway stations, at water buffalo in the rice paddies, at the timeless agricultural foreground and mountain background, all bathed in sunshine.

In Canton, after an hour of phoning, I reached Dr. Frank, professor of chemistry at Lingnam University. A family friend, he graciously invited us to stay at his home at the university until we could secure reservations on the train for Changsha, the site of Yale-in-China. We found ourselves housed in immaculate rooms in a brick residence, treated as honored guests, and introduced during our stay of four days to other members of the faculty, among them Dr. F. A. McClure, botanist, who initiated us into some of the complexities of identifying hundreds of species of bamboo, his specialty, and acquainted us with the captivating unfamiliar bird songs and interesting ferns found on campus — some of them, to my amazement, familiar from their New England counterparts.

At bedtime on our second night the air-raid alarm went off, reminding us that China was at war and that her cities were cruelly vulnerable. Dr. McClure, John, and I went out and sat on the lawn where we could follow by ear a solitary Japanese bomber, a single Chinese pursuit plane, and the sound of evasive action by the bomber. We heard gunfire, but the Chinese plane appeared to lose the bomber and then to search the sky for it. I thought I heard bombs at 12:30 when I went to bed. The morning news had it that eight bombers had been kept off and had come no closer to us than ten miles.

The war itself was one of the major phases of Japan's long-term plan for economic and military penetration of the mainland: establishment of control over Korea early in the century, over the adjacent Manchurian provinces in 1931, and over the area around Peiping in the summer of 1937, just as John and I were on our way out to China.

Every experience those days was a first. We had persimmons for breakfast along with our Grapenuts, scrambled eggs, and coffee. I learned how

9

to deal with a pomelo, removing the pear-shaped grapefruit rind, dividing up the interior, splitting open and turning inside out each moon-shaped section to get at the edible flesh—quickly and permanently a favorite fruit. That day at the Canton waterfront, a sobering first: the corpse of a coolie floating under the bridge at the Foreign Concession, later moored fifty yards downstream by a string attached to one of his ankles.

In the early evening the next air-raid siren went off. With lights out and supper postponed, we shortly discovered three bombers in formation coming from the west with their lights on. They flew toward the airfield about a mile and a half away, and we heard the bombs. We could see flashes from the gun of the lone pursuit plane. The antiaircraft guns didn't begin until we could no longer hear the bombers, which were probably by then on their way back to base on Taiwan (Formosa). Our fears over these early raids were partly that they would cut the rail connection to Changsha, a line which had been completed only in the previous year. One of the important arteries to Central China, it was about four-hundred miles long, took a day and a half to cover; and was our only practical means of getting to Hunan. Due to various unavoidable delays, we had already missed the opening of school and the beginning of classes.

Learning that Canton had more than four thousand cases of cholera, we went for shots. Further, we bought for use on the train tea, rice, tinned foods, pomelos, and bananas. At the Canton station, after a chaotic time getting all our luggage onto the train by 8 p.m., the air-raid siren blew, lights went out, and we waited, expecting that the station itself might be bombed. We heard no planes; our train finally left about an hour late. Although it averaged less than fifteen miles an hour, it kept more or less continuously in motion and methodically ate up the miles northward. We were lucky to be in first class. The train, possessing no second, had most of its passengers in third, where they attempted to sleep, either six to a compartment or sprawled in the day coaches at all angles and in frightful congestion.

We watched the hills and rice paddies of Kwangtung give way to similar Hunan countryside. We chatted with an Italian, pleasant and

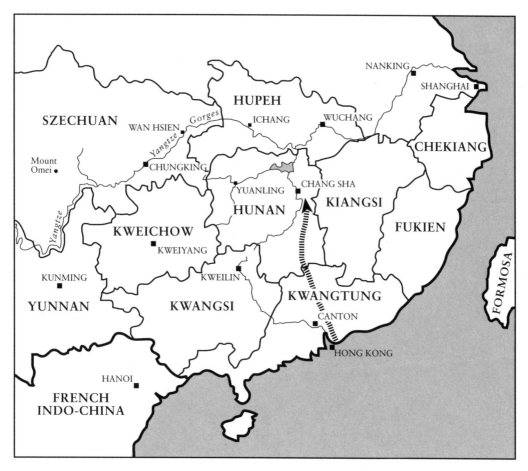

Central and South China

friendly, and with an affable Chinese, the chief wireless operator for
China Central News Agency. The Chinese, in a friendly attempt to
enhance our spare diet, ordered a dozen boiled eggs for us from the
steward. I couldn't imagine why he bought so many until he began to
open them. One after another was vividly and aromatically rotten; all
had to be thrown out. We napped successfully, waking to one of our
good pomelos, but our second night was again sleepless, as we fretted
about the uncertainties of the next two years. The train, several hours
late, planted us in Changsha about 10 a.m. on Monday, September 20, to

be met by Ying K'ai-shih, dean of the Yali Union school, Burton Rogers, head of the English Department, and our two colleagues, Sid Sweet and Minotte Chatfield, both Yale 1936. We solved our baggage problems, rickshawed to the school and our new home, the Bachelors' mess, where smiles of servants and neighbors and a celebratory round of firecrackers greeted our arrival.

At Yali

We arrived in Central China near the end of an era of devastating dislocation and political confusion. To many, it is best symbolized by the warlord, a figure that flourished throughout China during the era of disintegrated central authority between the collapse of the Ch'ing dynasty (the Manchus) in 1911 and the rebuilding of a centralized national structure — first by the Nanking government in the late 1920s and then more completely by the Communists from 1949 on. Depending upon the particular part of China, there was a characteristic period of two or more decades after the demise of the Manchus, during which governmental authority was hopelessly fragmented, and the local bosses and bullies, the warlords, took over. They varied enormously in power, sometimes controlling as much as an entire province; often, no more than a county or two; perhaps only a city and its agricultural environs. With an economic base in taxing power or rice harvests or opium production, they printed local money and had their own armies.

To overcome the tremendous disadvantages — both domestic and international — of this atomized body politic, Chiang Kai-shek — the disciple of Sun Yat Sen, China's premier republican revolutionary — undertook in 1926 to march from South China into the power centers of Central China, with the aim of unifying all of China under a new Nationalist government.

By the time of my arrival in China in 1937, this process of consolidation had been generally successful, in fact so successful that it had become one of the causes of the Japanese invasion of China that had just begun in the summer months.

The historical context of 1937 was of enhanced importance in a less obvious sense. We had gone to the other side of the world in the 1930s for reasons related to mission history. In the nineteenth century the Christian missionary had construed his work as primarily and almost exclusively evangelical. Protestant mission boards in London and Boston had sent men to remote parts of the world to preach the Gospel. They were expected to learn the language, translate the scripture, make converts, and build congregations. The Apostle Paul was their chief model — traveler, preacher, inspirer, sojourner. Essential to the process was the training of local talent within the congregation to take over the work of the expanding Church, so the missionary could move on.

Although missionaries in that era varied in talent and spirituality, as a group they characteristically exhibited intense motivation, attitudes of cultural superiority, and religious aggressiveness. They did not question, as we would today, the appropriateness of grafting a European religion onto the diverse cultures of Africa, Asia, and the Pacific. But along with their condescension and disruptive assertions they also brought the stimuli of brotherly love, criticism, and new ideas.

As missionaries developed understanding of the complex cultures they both served and buffeted, they accommodated more to them, softening and diversifying their message through the invention of medical missions and the addition of educational institutions. By the beginning of the twentieth century those two processes were well advanced in selected coastal areas of China. Identifying itself with them, Yale-in-China had become a leader in both medical and educational missions in the interior, its work concentrated in Changsha, the capital of Hunan province. Although profoundly Christian in motivation, Yale-in-China's goal was not to evangelize, but to be of help by supplying education, medical assistance, and medical training. Thus, the religious atmosphere at Yali was that of the social gospel — helping the Hunanese at a difficult time in their history by doing useful and practical things for them, as good samaritans.

The stance of Yali and Hsiang Ya (the medical side) was that westernized education and Western medicine had legitimate roles to play in

China, but they required Western personnel to get them started; and that Chinese, as they were trained, would gradually take over as teachers, administrators, doctors and nurses. By 1937 the process in Hsiang Ya had been complete for several years. Chinese personnel had been trained and were effectively in charge, holding the top positions and filling most of the others.

Some positions at Yali and Hsiang Ya were still held by American missionaries. Frank Hutchins represented the New Haven office and the Yale-in-China trustees; Dwight Rugh served as chaplain to the several dozen Christian students; Burton Rogers was head of the English Department. Phil Greene and Edna Hutchinson were, respectively, head of surgery and dean of the nursing school. These were all dedicated Christians, rather unemotional and undemonstrative, each a professional in his field, each devoting years of first-rate service to our school and hospital. The Yali Bachelors, as we four teachers were called, rounded out that group, and were essentially cast in the same mold. All the rest of the staff was Chinese.

Of the Bachelors, John Runnalls and Sid Sweet were devout, orthodox Christians; Minotte Chatfield and I were unenthusiastic churchgoers, both having less clearly defined, more eclectic religious attitudes than the Episcopalianism of the other two. I felt comfortable with the usefulness of our work, its emphasis on service and Christian witness, and that was what, for me, legitimized my doubting presence there. I couldn't have formulated my religious stance very well. It had been shaped by my mother's identification in Wellesley with the Congregational church and my attendance at Sunday school. Later, at Phillips Andover, I had been exposed to and impressed by the Sunday sermons of a revolving group of brilliant churchmen who traveled around among the New England prep schools and Ivy League colleges. I loved my school's Sunday Vespers at five o'clock, with the repetitive cadences of the prayers and responses. I loved the Christmas story. I loved the opening Psalm at Camp Lanakila in the summer: "I will lift up mine eyes unto the hills. . . ." For me, God was usually linked with the out-of-doors.

I had the usual uncertainties. I was baffled over why the existence of God didn't lend itself to convincing rational proof. To me, religion was not what you professed so much as what you *did*, how you lived your life, how you acted, how close you brought your actions to what you

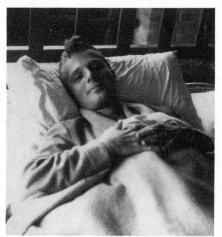

Left: The author, Edward Gulick, Yale '37, aged 22.

Right: Sidney Sweet, Yale '36, ill with jaundice on upstairs sleeping porch of Bachelors' mess; Sid came from a church family in St. Louis.

professed. It was more important to be honest than to profess honesty; indeed professing it might then be irrelevant. To put it another way, your actions were themselves a living definition of what you really believed. Since Confucianism inculcated the identity of philosophy and the living of one's life, I was unwittingly quite Chinese in my stance.

I came from a family which had played a prominent role in Protestant missions in the nineteenth and early twentieth centuries. My great-grandfather, Peter Gulick, had been a pioneer missionary in the Sandwich Islands, and his many children had played active and sometimes prominent roles in the Congregational church and for the American Board of Commissioners for Foreign Missions, chiefly in Hawaii, Micronesia, and Japan. My grandfather lived and worked in Japan, and my father lived there as a boy. My mother grew up in Turkey, the daughter of a Canadian missionary who served the American Board in the late nineteenth century as the principal of a boys' school in Constantinople.

Despite these forebears, I disliked old-fashioned missionary evangelism and was positively embarrassed when a young man sought me out for religious instruction so that he could become a Christian.

Among the four of us the two Senior Bachelors, Sid Sweet and Minotte

Chatfield, were beginning the second year of their contracts; John Runnalls and I were the Junior Bachelors, just embarking on our first. We were all part of an artfully designed system which had been in operation for twenty-five years or so and which had sent several dozen young Yale graduates out for two memorable years apiece. The conception was that Yali's small group of long-term foreign staff members — Frank Hutchins, Dwight Rugh, and Burton Rogers in my era — would be supplemented by four, recent, Yale graduates on overlapping, two-year contracts. The Senior Bachelors would have the fun of helping to break in the Juniors, and the school would benefit from the freshness and enthusiasm of two new Bachelors each fall.

Our travel was paid to and from China, and we received a monthly salary of $33 U.S. and $100 Mex (that is, Chinese dollars, each worth about thirty cents U.S. in 1937). The stipend was small by American standards but ample for household expenses and travel in Central China at that time.

Since virtually no Chinese language or Chinese history were taught in the U.S. in that era, we Bachelors were innocent of both when we arrived

Left: John Runnalls, Yale classmate with whom I traveled from Europe to Hong Kong; seen here (white shirt) during hiatus at Suez, August 1937.

Right: Minotte Chatfield, Yale '36, son of a New Haven businessman, here with our neighbors Ellen and Fritz Greene on lawn of Bachelors' mess.

at Yali. With no credentials beyond B.A.'s and our general willingness, we nevertheless, as a group, effectively fitted into the ongoing life of the Middle School.

Much of this was due to the skill and tact of our superiors, Frank and Burton, but the real keys to our successful participation were the twin oddities that we knew English and that English was crucial for our students. Not just important, but crucial. By 1937 China had built up a westernized educational system of colleges, universities, medical schools, and engineering schools faster than its scholars had been able to write textbooks in Chinese. The result was that those institutions used available texts, which happened to be in English. Because American editions were too expensive for Chinese students, some Shanghai firms pirated them on cheap paper, the American author being unprotected by copyright in China. For these bizarre, transient reasons, our English classes at Yali were highly useful. The atmosphere was purposeful; there was fun, too, but no nonsense, since we had much to accomplish.

Our Bachelor's household, a part of this tested Yali pattern, consisted of Sid — socially poised, amiable, tennis-playing; Chat — more informal, a roughhouser, liked by our younger students; John — football player and raconteur; and me — history and literature buff. Energetic and athletic, enthusiastic, given to bursts of hilarity, we proved eminently congenial.

Different households had weekly teas on set days of the week; ours were held on Thursdays. Before guests arrived for our first November tea, Ta Ssu-fu, the cook, put a large cake on the dining room table. It looked wonderful with its thick vanilla frosting, and soon all four of us were standing around the cake admiring its lines and thinking discreditable thoughts. With mock dignity we decided that its rectangularity enabled us to remove a middle row of four pieces and slide the divided parts of the cake together to heal the schism. We did this, loving the cake. We tapped it a bit here and there to effect a perfect disguise of our perfidy. Those were happy weeks as we were getting to know each other. They were yet unmarred by the war's disasters.

· · ·

The faculty residences were clustered in a stretch of several hundred feet between the edge of the soccer field and the north compound wall at the rear of the campus. Our Bachelors' mess was typical of these residences. One approached this red-brick structure by sidewalk, terrace, and lawn. The first floor interior of conventional American rooms had dark paneling, a jumbled, uninviting library, a large living room with stove and slightly run-down furniture like that in a fraternity house, and a screened porch with ping pong table. Upstairs there were three medium-sized bedrooms, two sleeping porches, and a bathroom with cold running water (not to be drunk), a bottle of potable water for use with toothbrushes, and a toilet box, the contents of which were removed daily, for use in farming, by a special, nightsoil coolie, the humblest of the labor hierarchy. Hot water canisters were brought upon request by the Number Two or Number Three servants. There was no cellar, and what attic there was, was not used.

A doorway from the dining room opened directly into the kitchen and

Bachelors' mess: entrance up the brick walk, single-story servants' quarters to the left, one of our two upstairs verandahs visible on right — crucial for sleeping comfort in the hot weather. Superficially, the house could have been in an English or American middle-class suburb.

the domain of the servants. Our taciturn cook prepared standard American meals for breakfast and dinner, with Chinese fare for lunch. He was consistently better at the American than the Chinese, which seemed odd to me until one of our Chinese friends pointed out that the cook made more "squeeze" out of his shopping for the American meals.

He cooked with crumbly coal held together with clay and water, the mixture being plastered within the throat of the little firepit that served as a stove. He made that operation look frightfully simple; but I now think it was wonderfully precise and skilled.

He was Number One and commanded a salary of $20 Mex a month, plus perquisites. Number Two, a more ebullient individual, handled the waiting-on with immense cheerfulness, did the beds and cleaning, the laundry, and some of the shopping. I never fathomed the mystery of his soap, but, after Tseng Ssu-fu had laundered our shirts for several months, you could have plucked them apart with chopsticks. Number Three usually carried the hot water and did the errands which were often time-consuming due to the general absence of telephones. One of the Bachelors, in our case Sidney, traditionally ran the household, supervised the servants, paid them, conferred with the cook about meals, saw that invitations were sent out to our teas and parties, and submitted bills to the other Bachelors for their monthly share of the household expenses. The recipients, ingrates that we were, were more apt to grumble over the bill than thank our manager for his efforts. Anyone who grumbled too much, however, ran the risk of inheriting the task forthwith.

The faculty residences seemed to me an exception to the appropriateness of the school's architecture. Although their Victorian equals existed in abundance in Britain and America, and although we would probably be living in comparable structures at home in the States, they were out of scale in Central China in the 1930s; they could too easily be stereotyped as symbols of the arrogant, too-rich foreigner. We had more space than the typical Changsha family; the buildings were higher than was customary in the city; and there was the implication of our distancing ourselves from the Chinese whom we sought to serve. Actually the Bachelors were less distanced from the students than was the Chinese staff; nevertheless those buildings invited criticism and were an inappropriate and risky indulgence for Yali. They symbolized the high period of mission activity in China.

Yali's Setting

Yali was at the northern end of Changsha, a riverine port, commercial center, and capital of a relatively rich province of thirty million people. It was an old city, dingy, gray, undistinguished in architecture, and with a population estimated at five hundred thousand. Walled for many centuries, possibly even millennia, the city had recently seen most of its ancient and dilapidated wall torn down and thriftily converted into a circumferential road to relieve the narrow streets of the inner city of some of the congestion of rickshaws, porters, and pedestrians. The broad new road allowed the occasional auto and public bus of the autumn of 1937 an unaccustomed maneuverability.

Seen from the Island, residential exclave of the foreign business community in the north-flowing Hsiang River, Changsha presented just a long, straight waterfront facade, low and flat. Like Shakespearean London, much of the city's action took place on the water. The river was constantly alive with sampans, the small craft used as ferries for the bridgeless river, or junks, the more capacious and clumsier-looking workhorse craft on which the owner and his family lived.

To a walker or bicyclist the city first revealed itself as an animated congestion of pedestrians, rickshaws, wheelbarrows and porters, all crowded into a maze of gray, narrow, twisting streets devoid of sewers. The granite slab, which was used by the thousands to pave those streets, was undoubtedly a great and useful urban invention; but the bicycle seat, the bumpy slab-to-slab junctures, and male anatomy were, and remain, uncompromisingly uncongenial.

I was struck by the clustering of stores, say six or eight tinsmiths forming a small neighborhood group of their own; by the compactness of individual shops, each with removable wooden shutters, an apprentice making something in the storefront, the master inside, living quarters in the rear or up one flight on the top floor — manufacture, sale, and residence all neatly packaged. Where stores did not line the treeless streets one was perpetually confronted by walls, blank walls of stone or brick, ten to twenty feet high. In time I realized that these were residential walls of the well-to-do, to be penetrated only through a deceptively dingy door presided over by a gruff gatekeeper. If one was lucky enough to enter the door, there might be a number of connected courtyards, each open to the sky, each surrounded by one-story rooms and dwellings.

One was aware of crowds, of talkativeness, of the noisy clang of rickshaw bells and the shouts of porters wanting clear passage, of the occasional whiff of opium and the click of mah jong, both illegal in the puritanism of the New Life Movement (the code of civic rectitude put forward by the Nanking government).

John and I celebrated the completion of our first month in Changsha by going to visit Rocky Chin (just arrived from Hong Kong) at a school across the river where he had secured a temporary teaching job. We then planned to climb Yo-lo Shan (Mount Yolo). We bused to the other end of the city, visited a Buddhist temple, and took the ferry. The river was lovely, as was our walk to the monastery where we located Rocky. We hiked up the mountain with him and a couple of his students, pausing for splendid views en route. We went in a religious progression from a large Confucian temple at the base, past a Buddhist establishment halfway up in a grove of trees, to a Taoist temple on top. The three in combination were often used to symbolize the ready eclecticism of the Chinese, who freely visited all three when hiking on the mountain.

This, my first view of the city from above, came on a day of golden sunshine. It was astonishing to discover that Changsha, that cobblestone desert, treeless and grassless to the pedestrian within the city, was, when seen from above, a relatively green city, its drabness and harshness dramatically modified by the now-visible courtyard trees and shrubs.

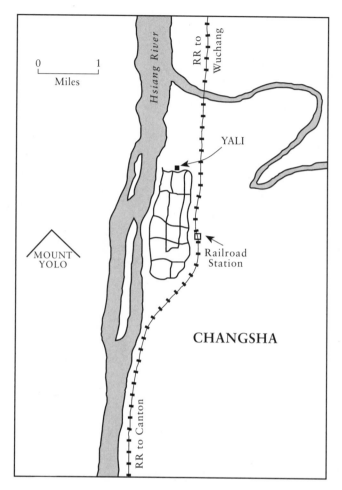

Changsha. Yali campus was at the north end of the city, a short walk east of the river. Changsha was a compact city up to the point where, without transition, it suddenly became total farmland.

It was also astonishing to look away from river and city into the characteristic high hill country of Hunan with pampas grass on treeless slopes, with hilltop profiles exquisitely sharp against the sunset, and row upon row of water-color-flattened hills in ever lighter grays as they receded towards the horizon. Chinese artists for over a thousand years had found these flat grays irresistible.

Yo-lo Shan, seen in the sunlight and from the Yali campus, was green, dark or light by patches; in the mist it could be brown or gray; in the

23

Yo-lo Shan (Mount Yolo) — treeless, rounded, eroded — was on the west side of the Hsiang River, several miles southwest of the Yali campus.

evening it was gray to black, the gray uniform except for the slightly darker quality at the top. In the spring there were abundant yellow and red azaleas on its slopes. To me, the mountain's beauty made up for the scenic qualities that the city itself lacked.

·　　·　　·

An immediate part of our setting at Yali was the countryside, to which our location gave virtually instant access. John and I went with Edna Hutchinson on a bicycle trip east toward the Little River with Edna's uninhibited dog, Hans, as a free-wheeling outrider. Hans, at full gallop, stepped on a distracted chicken, routed herons from classic poses in the rice fields, and tilted with "wonks," Central China's repulsive dogs. We turned off the road onto the paths between the rice paddies and took a long trip into the most tranquil, timeless countryside I had ever visited. It could have been the time of the Han dynasty. We stopped to watch farmers at work in the fields and passed men taking pigs to market. The scream of the outraged hogs, tightly trussed to wheelbarrows, together with the shriek of ungreased wooden wheels, sounded one of the characteristic chords of autumnal Hunan. We examined an arrangement where a water buffalo circled under a straw shelter, drawing water into the rice fields. The mechanism, its wooden parts carefully and efficiently assembled, represented a very old technology.

Colors in the landscape were dominated by the extravagant combination of red soil, green foliage, and blue sky. Smoke lingered about groups of houses. We visited a little temple which had been partly converted to a store, around which quickly gathered interesting and interested faces, all concentrating on us. They stared and we stared back, in neutrality but also with intense curiosity. I soon discovered how typical it was for twenty or more to gather within a minute. Mutual staring was fair enough, save that they outnumbered us exponentially. It was not like an early Christian being thrown to the lions, but eventually cumulative stare-fatigue set in. Within the city, one could retain a sense of privacy by traveling in a ricksha, but that was both too inactive and somewhat embarrassing. For a trip into the countryside the bicycle offered double blessings. It gave us exercise and enabled us to get away from the inevitable starers.

The rice fields we passed in that season were generally drained for the ripening of the grain and the impending harvest. Whatever the crop, the farm fields were hedgeless, weedless, neat, compact, carefully thought out in terms of companion crops and succession of crops. Obviously tended by skilled hands, whether of owners or tenants, they appeared highly productive. Tiny farm ponds about half the size of a tennis court were commonly used to raise fish.

Characteristic also were the night-soil pits near the edges of the fields with green human manure being seasoned before being ladled out onto the fields. The stench was powerful enough to drive out the Mongols. Not only that, but fly larvae bred in the pits by unimaginable trillions. One of the most unnerving minor experiences was to drop a stone into an apparently lifeless night-soil pit and watch the surface quiver and heave from the shoals of larvae wriggling in their putrid stew. The pits were thus part of a devastating communications network for intestinal diseases, which flourished in the night soil and were moved about by the emerging swarms of flies.

But on the positive side, as I learned, the night soil had been crucial in maintaining the fertility of these fields for dozens of centuries, a very impressive agricultural feat. Traditional Chinese agriculture was often dismissed by Western specialists with lofty remarks about the need for artificial fertilizers, pesticides, and costly machinery. However, judged in terms of energy-input and energy-harvest, with *all* major items figured in, the traditional Chinese system shows a net gain, while the typical Midwestern cornfield shows a net loss.

On another occasion we took a captivating trip into the hills. November 15 was one of those days blessed by the gods, with the sun burning through an early mist to produce a clear sky and warm weather, just right for our proposed bicycle trip to Ku Shan, a small mountain across the river and about two hours' ride into the countryside. All four of the Bachelors went along, escorting Edna and a friend and escorted by Edna's dog Hans. As soon as we had ferried the river by sampan, John and I were initiated into the intense concentration involved in bicycling the tortuous paths between fields where rice still stood in mud under sheets of water in some of the paddies.

The rice paddies were skillfully terraced, the water held in each by meticulously maintained embankments of soil, turf, and stone. Since drainage between the paddies required small channels under the paths, there were long narrow stones not more than eight inches wide which served as tiny culvert bridges for pedestrians, cyclists, and wheelbarrow wheels. We had to get our wheels squarely onto dozens and dozens of these narrows and cross them rapidly to keep up. The game of steering was further complicated by the free-flowing scorn of our friends if one's foot touched the ground in the interest of avoiding a humiliating plunge into a rice paddy. Although the path was never straight for more than a hundred feet, we somehow made our way through with only an occasional sneaky footfault.

We pulled up at a temple at the foot of the mountain, left our bikes and retired to a nearby grove of giant bamboo for lunch and tea served by one of the monks. Those hillside bamboos were the means for my

EVG riding the bamboo down.

pursuing a time-honored Bachelors' sport—namely, climbing high on the bamboo, then, with a firm grip, swinging my legs out and riding the deeply flexing trunk to a drop-off point near the ground. It was exciting and enchanting. Robert Frost should have been there.

One is constantly aware of bamboo in China, its uncounted uses ranging from dippers, waterpipes, drains, and reinforcements, through eating bamboo shoots with bamboo chopsticks, to chairs, mats, woven ropes, toys, and instruments of torture. Botanically extraordinary, bamboo exists in hundreds of species that vary from pencil to flagpole thickness, and which may blossom only at intervals of thirty years or more. Whatever the age of individual plants in the region, and whatever the irregular interval since the last blossoming, when they do blossom,

27

Edna Hutchinson (University of California at Los Angeles) B.A. 1930; Yale School of Nursing, R.N. 1935. Athletic, devout, active, Edna is here shown on one of our forays into the Hunan countryside. The parallel stone-faced tracks are not for autos, but for two-way wheelbarrow traffic. Rice fields lie fallow after the harvest.

Edna, dean of the nursing school, was a wonderful companion on these outings. Here she is threshing a double handful of rice stalks into a bin in one of the world's simplest and oldest modes of harvesting grain.

Typical of our forays into the countryside outside Changsha: we on bicycles; the Chinese moving vegetables to market via wheelbarrow, shoulder harness, and manpower.

all blossom simultaneously, as when a caravan stops for evening prayers the camels all urinate in concert.

The trunk and leaves of the bamboo lend themselves to the calligraphic brush strokes of China's great watercolor tradition, inviting celebration of its beauty in painting, often heavily loaded with symbolism. In the treasured image of traditional Chinese culture bamboo stood for the Confucian gentleman, the perfect scholar-courtier, flexible and strong, bending to the storm but superbly unbroken.

We hiked quickly up the mountain, and sat in the sun in a warm saucer-like spot at the summit, looking out over uncounted Hunan hills.

The "China Stare" — the instant assembly of neutral, staring bystanders whenever one paused in village or city.

We ferried home across the river at dusk, the western sky alight with orange-yellow behind the darkening mountains, each ridge a different gray; the river was quieting down, a few junks still under sail — an enchanted end to a happy day. We were home shortly for hot baths and a big supper. Each of these day trips, however modest its objective, was an adventure for me, brimming with new sights and sounds. Each helped me to perceive the province and approach an understanding of it.

·   ·   ·

As our days continued to unfold in an absorbing miscellany of newness and friendly contacts, they were very soon accompanied by a nagging uncertainty over how much longer we would be in Changsha. Changsha was about the same distance from the Japanese as Hankow, which had been badly bombed since our arrival; this meant to us that we might be next. Chat thought we would have to leave in less than six months; Sid, that we would be bombed soon; I, that the Japanese would mainly concentrate on what they had already undertaken in eastern China. A cable from Dick Weigle, executive secretary of the Yale-in-China home office, assured us that evacuation from Changsha was possible, if desired. He added the congratulations of the Trustees for our devotion in staying on the job, and suggested the construction of air-raid shelters. So preoccupied was I with my classroom tasks, with the fascination of everything around me, that the thought of leaving the school, or moving it, was quite beyond my comprehension.

In mid-October Edna, John, and I bicycled several miles out of the city to the Widow's P'ai-lou, a memorial arch celebrating prolonged devotion within widowhood. We explored the hillside trenches, played with Hans and enjoyed the ravishing shades of green in the landscape on the other side of the river. On our return the air-raid warning blew for the first time since our arrival. We fluttered about, wondering what to do in case of an actual raid. We had agreed, if need be, to get under the new ping-pong table after piling chairs and sofas around it. Our rationale was that we especially needed protection from debris falling on us, if the house was bombed. It is embarrassing to record how unrealistic we were, but in the autumn of 1937 most of the world was understandably inexperienced in dealing with the new menace of air raids. No planes came this time.

The fantastic miscellany of that autumn in Changsha continued: an evening was devoted to a talk by Mr. Tseng Po-sun and his cousin Tseng Pao-sun at Dwight's house on the perplexing relation of a Christian to war. I was impressed by the clarity of their minds and the thoughtfulness of their low-key remarks. It was only much later that I learned that these were the grandchildren of Tseng Kuo-fan, China's pre-eminent statesman in the nineteenth century. Friends of Yali, they were themselves educators, having started the I-Fang Middle School for Girls in the garden of their ancestral courtyards near North Gate Street in Changsha.

The next day I handed back the VI-i exams and spent much of the hour on them; after class I joined some of the boys for conversation on the grass outside. I told them about my trip out, forgetting my own language lesson. When I got home, I found T'ang Hsien-sheng, the Bachelors' charming and long-suffering language teacher, contentedly looking over the last copy of the *New Yorker*. He and I, unhappily, operated on very different wave lengths. Whereas the others all seemed to benefit from his language instruction, I was totally at sea without theoretical explanations, which he was unable to offer.

At our weekly tea Dr. Fabel, a German economist who lived in Changsha, told us that he thought the city would be bombed very soon. In token anticipation of that possibility, shelters for students were being excavated, some of them in the bank at the edge of our front yard. The simultaneous digging of a cesspool for the Bachelors' mess was halfway toward completion. Soon we would be able to boast one of the few flush toilets in the province. Again the jangling miscellany.

A welcome escape from air-raid talk was offered by our hectic preparations for the annual Bachelors' Halloween party. John and Chat cleaned up the living room, piling accumulated books and papers in a heap in the study. They fixed up the lighting system and installed a ghostly figure in the corner with a pumpkin head, which one of our servants was to raise and lower with a cord from John's room above. Sid busied himself with carving the pumpkins, while I hastily drew a poster-size Japanese general and cut out several tails that the guests, blindfolded, were expected to pin on his ample posterior. The decorations over one of the front room lights burst into flames, and all the lights went out. But Yankee ingenuity prevailed and we got them back before our thirty-five Chinese and foreign guests began to arrive.

Each new guest was welcomed in dim light by John ("Do you swear to see the ghost, the whole ghost, and nothing but the ghost?") and greeted with Sid's sepulchral handshake — his imitation red hand coming right off, to squeals of delight. Our welcoming song was a three-voice barbershop desecration of "We Three Kings of Orient Are" with the words:

> We three spooky Bachelors be
> welcoming you to join in our spree
> on our brooms we come from tombs,
> moaning mournfully, Oh . . . !
> You'll see witches, you'll see ghosts,
> don't know which will scare you most
> groaning, moaning, round you roaming
> with your blood we'll drink a toast.

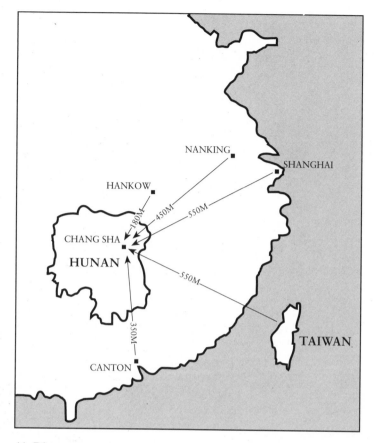

Air Distances

Pure corn, greeted with fervid applause. The cultural mismatch appeared to bother no one.

The Japanese general was sensationally successful, as was a game where competitors of opposite sexes began chewing at either end of a piece of string, trying to arrive first at the candy tied in the middle. "No hands" meant plenty of aggressive body action, often ending on knees on the floor, the Bachelor face to face with an enthusiastic, actively chewing, usually dignified Chinese girl or matron. Laughter wiped out whatever international barriers the guests may have brought with them. Our cook's pumpkin and lemon pies were excellent; a humdrum cook during the week, he always rose to special occasions.

33

Our tutor, T'ang Hsien-sheng (i.e., Mr. T'ang). Many of the Bachelors enjoyed this man, who taught an unabashed Hunanese pronunciation and dialect by direct method.

34

Our guests declared over and over again that it was the best party of its kind ever given. When they dispersed soon after ten — many with appreciable distances to be covered on foot or by rickshaw — we Bachelors sat down to liberate some of the remaining pie. This developed into our first real bull session. It lasted until 1 a.m., ending with a well-told tale from John about a New London racing weekend with his drunken skipper creating havoc among the arrogant craft of the Newport set. We had come together nicely as a Bachelor family.

The School

The Yali Union Middle School combined the junior high and high school years (i.e., ages 13–15 and 16–18) for about 450 Chinese boys. Founded about thirty years earlier, staffed with a well-trained Chinese faculty and administration, and committed generally to preparing students for university work, Yali had become one of the outstanding secondary schools in China. Its campus of twenty acres stood on the north edge of Changsha, one half mile east of the river and about one mile from the railroad station. There were various structures — a gatehouse, science lab, dormitory, dining room, a long low classroom building, a chapel which served also as an assembly hall, a small music building near the chapel, and eight residences for faculty and administration.

The school buildings were straightforward red brick, one-story and two-story structures, with upturned roof corners. More Western than Eastern but not obnoxiously alien. The same foreign flavor was suggested by the shape and conception of the residences, their lawns and flower gardens, and the green turf of the soccer field.

There was the usual compound wall, in this case part stone and part wood. Later strengthened, its presence made a difference when the Japanese occupied the city, an event hardly dreamed of in the fall of 1937. The gatehouse, with its modest living arrangements for gatekeeper and family, opened onto the Yali Malo, a wide, unpaved road with moderate pedestrian and wheelbarrow traffic, but virtually no cars.

Directly across the Malo was the gatehouse for the compound containing the Hsiang Ya Hospital, the medical school and nursing school, dorms, and faculty residences.

The classroom buildings and dormitories were sturdy and utilitarian, with conventional American windows, a few electrical outlets, cold running water with hot to be had in a bucket, if requested; but with no heating and no flush toilets. A not very large staff of servants kept the facility running smoothly.

All in all, the architectural layout seems to me to have been serviceable but not gaudy; I think it struck the right note. It made the point that we were an untraditional school, serving Central China but not wholly of it, training the sons of establishment families (many also from modest backgrounds) and yet brash enough to raise un-Chinese educational questions and to suggest a set of partly Westernized answers. Since I had attended an establishment prep school in New England, I felt an immediate identification with Yali's intense commitment to training able boys for positions of leadership. Although Phillips Andover had resources a hundredfold—a thousandfold—more substantial than Yali, their common ground was recognizable.

The Hsiang Ya Hospital was one of the chief enterprises of Yale-in-China. It had been founded in 1911 as a means of meeting one of the most evident needs of Hunan province, at that time without any hospital for its population of thirty million. Since the ideal of the Yale-in-China Mission was to initiate work and then turn it over to a trained Chinese staff, both medical and nursing schools, each with over a hundred students, became necessary adjuncts to the hospital. Many of the Yali Middle School graduates crossed the street to the Medical College, and some ultimately joined the Hsiang Ya staff.

A B.A. was not a prerequisite to medicine. Having had middle school training in the sciences, the student went directly into medical school, the first year or two being basic premed. From the Chinese perspective, much of the standard lab drill in American medical and premed training appeared irrelevant, needlessly costly, elitist, and wasteful of time. The Chinese system has, ever since its medical missionary phase, avoided many of these weaknesses. This was true of our Hsiang Ya complex of doctors, nurses, trainees, technicians, and servants—together compris-

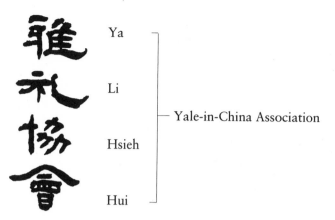

Ya

Li

Hsieh

Hui

— Yale-in-China Association

The two Chinese characters comprising the name Ya-li were taken from a line in the *Analects*, one of the basic Confucian classics. There the characters emphasize Confucius as teacher, referring to his lecturing "with elegance" (Ya) on *The Book of Songs*, *The Book of History*, and the meticulous observance of "etiquette" (Li). "Li" played a major role in traditional Chinese education, where the pupil was expected to absorb a code of gentlemanly conduct that underscored personal propriety as the way to civic harmony.

Profile of Hsiang Ya Hospital (center) in the deep background. In front of it Yali's main, one-story recitation building; science building, dormitory, and chapel are out of the picture, but close by on the left. In the foreground is athletic field with a giant puddle of water reflecting the outsize magpies' nest high in the tree.

39

ing as trim and well-integrated a medical endeavor as is likely to be found anywhere.

The hospital itself, a large structure of red brick and reinforced concrete, had been built in World War I with assistance from Edward S. Harkness, a generous benefactor of Yale University. Opened in 1917, it normally could handle two hundred inpatients and from two hundred to four hundred outpatients in the daily clinics. There were a few private rooms, but most inpatients were in the wards, which were actively used in the teaching program for both student doctors and nurses.

The student nurses were exclusively young women, and therefore not products of our Middle School. The medical students, interns, and residents were both male and female. They were much more radical in certain ways than their American counterparts in that era — their commitment to Western medicine was an act of radicalism in a part of China where traditional medical work was overwhelmingly nonsurgical, relying heavily on herbs, pulse theory, acupuncture, and moxibustion (a blister therapy). Their participation in coeducation was also radical in Hunan, although mission colleges had pioneered it in other parts of China a generation earlier. As late as my first autumn in Hunan one student, from a conservative background and with a scholar's long fingernails, withdrew from medical school rather than cut his nails to scrub for operations. My still totally American self found that astounding.

Students were forever involved in propaganda marches to publicize antiseptic procedures, the need to control the overwhelming fly population, or the like. They helped in the rural clinics conducted by Hsiang Ya doctors. They were latter-day, Central China pioneers of Western medicine, the scientific descendants of Dr. Peter Parker from Yale, who had done more than anyone else to implant medical missions in China. His Canton Hospital, begun in 1835, was his principal achievement. It was still in existence in 1937, although it had long since been surpassed by mission hospitals in other parts of China.

The medical service in the Hsiang Ya Hospital was superb. Performed with slender supplies and minimal drugs, it offered clean, simple, basic care in the wards with no frills, but with close scrutiny during rounds from doctors. The doctors, who were mostly Chinese, were the beneficiaries of repeated contact with a fantastic clinical spectrum of diseases.

What they lacked in equipment, they more than made up in the multiplicity of their clinical exposures to wide-ranging health conditions. I would hazard the proposition that the patient with a complex problem could get a quicker, surer diagnosis on the ward at Hsiang Ya in 1937 than in any of the great hospitals of Vienna, London, or Boston, to say nothing of the brilliance and reliability of Hsiang Ya's surgery, again from doctors who had scores of times coped with special problems that an eminent surgeon in the States might have encountered on only a few occasions.

And Hsiang Ya did it all on a shoestring.

．　　．　　．

Yali had a Chinese faculty of twenty or more, all married men, all well-trained university graduates knowledgeable in Chinese literature and classics, East Asian and Western history, math, science, art, government, and physical education. English, the one foreign language, was taught by the six Americans, who alone were able to put together a basketball team that easily led the Chinese faculty in the first half of a game and then was as easily beaten by the student team after the faculty stopped to save face.

Most of the Chinese staff were blandly eclectic in religion; some were active Christians, one of them ardently evangelical but alone in his belief that we all ought to devote an hour a day to proselytizing. They were intelligent men, generally in early middle age, most of them fluent in English, all actively participant in the westernized form of Chinese education that would prepare their students for the modern university training of that era.

It was a stable faculty with moderate turnover, a homogeneous group that got along well together. Faculty meetings had watermelon seeds, tea, and free discussion, often in English as a courtesy to us.

Slender and short by American standards, neither athletic nor interested in athletics, they were a good-looking group—healthy, smiling, seemingly unemotional, probably not highly imaginative. Although a few wore the traditional long gown of the scholar class, most wore Western garments. The long gown, although snug and efficient in winter time, was too restrictive for active men. To a considerable extent their dress symbolized ideological options and choices. They would have been

41

Dr. H. C. Chang, Head of Hsiang Ya Hospital and medical college. Member of Hsiang Ya's first graduating class of ten students in 1921.

Hsiang Ya Hospital, taken from the Yali Gate across the road. By turning right at the waiting rickshaw one had a ten-minute walk to the river.

"Students were forever involved in propaganda marches."

Dr. Greene and Rocky Chin, Yale Ph.D. in international relations.

scornful of the long fingernails and the precious estheticism of the old-fashioned scholar; been uneasy over the radicalism and disruptions of the local Communist movement; and accepting of the still lively, middle-class reformist tendencies of the Nanking government at the end of its first — and best — decade. Hence, few long gowns on campus, no peasant garbs, and many suitcoats, shirts, ties, and trousers. No faculty members seemed interested in elegance of dress, unless one regarded as such the overacceptance in that era of a Scott Fitzgerald felt hat. In the city one often saw the combination of traditional black cloth shoes and long gown, grandly topped off with a felt hat, unshaped and seated straight with no concession to jauntiness.

Not preoccupied with harsh thoughts about man's corruption, not much interested in self-denial or penitence, the faculty would have been better symbolized by the rationality and practicality of the abacus. They were an unsentimental group, neither self-destructively nostalgic nor self-pitying; not naively optimistic either, but conditioned to poise, balance, common sense, moderation, understatement; and blessed with a capacity for laughter in the ongoing wartime trauma of their personal and national lives.

Dignified and good disciplinarians in a quiet way, they were educators of bicultural sympathy, who believed in the formal classroom setting and were not given to chatty informalities with their students. After the Communist Revolution their teaching would become suspect in Mainland China, but I do not myself think of them as dogmatic or narrowly traditional. Yali had plenty of special dynamism of its own in its westernized curriculum and in its humane, civilized, and purposeful atmosphere of education. Within that framework, these men comprised an admirable faculty.

Our "mandarins" were Principal Lao and Dean Ying. The former had had a year or two of graduate work at Yale University, and was a conventional, but solid and effective, teacher. His field was mathematics, the most ecumenical of the sciences as far as Chinese scholars were concerned. Lao Ch'i-chiang fitted the implication of ecumenicism well because he retained a rather traditional outlook and at the same time could be fully involved in an intricate modern science. Compared to the dean, he made fewer compromises with the Occident, was less overtly westernized, and remained relatively critical of things American and

44

European. An individual of extreme pragmatism, he appeared to have little liking for ideas or the people who specialized in them; seemed distrustful of grand educational reforms and more at home with incremental changes, whose workability could be quickly tested. He had dignity and Face, but was neither as zestful a man nor as principled an educator as his dean. Affable, but a bit withdrawn too, he was Yali's most persistent alarmist and a devotee of the vibrant rumor mill.

The whole Yali enterprise was predicated on educating and training Chinese students, some of whom would themselves fill Yali's teaching and administrative positions and eventually take over the running of the school. Dean Ying was a stunning example of how that process worked.

The youngest son of a coal miner, Ying K'ai-shih had been sent, soon after the collapse of the Manchu dynasty, to the new missionary school (Yali), with his father's wish that he learn English but not get embroiled in Christianity. His acceptance at Yali had life-long consequences — good Middle School education led to a college degree (and Christianity), thence to teaching at Yali, graduate work in New Haven, and ultimately to becoming Dean of the Middle School, where he was tested to the utmost by the developing war crisis. We had no intimation, then, of the subsequent Communist relocation of Yali and of its absorption in the system of municipal schools, of the vilification of the dean for foreign ties and friends, and of his surviving this sea of troubles to be recognized — in a serene old age, free of bitterness — as one of China's outstanding educators. In 1937, much of that lay far ahead.

Mr. Ying had an M.A. in education from Yale and was an active dean, tops as a professional educator. Although he could be critical of the Occident, he was extremely understanding of differences in culture, as appreciative of new Western ways as of older Chinese modes, very good at interpreting America to Chinese students, and China to an American. One felt a close rapport with this practical, enthusiastic, sensible man, so interested in what was right and good, so very genuine, so sincere in his Christianity. On one occasion Mr. Ying was confronted by Burton, who had been absent when a guest speaker from the military addressed, at great length, a stand-up assembly: "What did the speaker have to say?" said Burton. Mr. Ying (with uncharacteristic vehemence): "Nothing! Absolutely nothing!"

Each different, Mr. Lao and Mr. Ying, the one suave and somewhat

remote, the other approachable, boyish, and bouncy, nicely comple-
mented each other's attributes; each carried responsibility well, the two
worked together smoothly, and jointly offered the school the outstanding leadership it needed during those years of Japan's disastrous invasion
of China. Yali was very lucky to have them.

· · ·

Our student body consisted of boys, ages twelve or thirteen to eighteen,
who were distributed more or less evenly among the six grades of junior
high and high school. They were exclusively Chinese. In appearance and
actuality they were a highly homogeneous group—that is, no intrusive
foreigners, no White Russians, no blondes, no redheads, no sense of the
polyglot coastal cities. They were, I'm sure, unanimous in such things as
the innate Chinese dislike of milk and milk products. We found that not
even a Chinese mouse would eat cheese.

The students also shared the uniformity of having handsome, excel-

Opposite left: Dwight Rugh, B.A. University of California 1921; with subsequent B.D. degree (ordained Congregational minister) and a Ph.D. in education and counseling. Dwight was a member of the permanent staff, an English teacher, and chaplain for the Christian students, who comprised a minority — but an active one — of the student body.

Opposite right: James Shen, our treasurer. A modest, soft-spoken, charming man, devoted to the well-being of the school. The file, the desk, the chair, the teacup, and the large abacus (seen just to the right of his shoulders) were his office equipment.

Above: Frank Hutchins, Oberlin B.A. 1925, staff member who handled liaison business between our school in Changsha and the home office in New Haven, spoke Chinese well, and was experienced in the ways of China.

Left: Mr. Chen Jen-lien, our physics teacher. A well-trained college graduate, quick, alert, and pleasant; good at teaching his subject without elaborate equipment; dressed in Western style; an ardent Christian.

Below: Mr. Cheng Ta-chiu, math teacher. The mathematics of Europe and of China flowed together into one ecumenical discipline, identical in East and West, during the seventeenth century when Jesuit fathers from Europe lived in Peking and were in touch with Chinese mathematicians.

Dean Ying

lent teeth, devoid of cavities and common Western dental problems, a condition which seemed true not only for our region, but generally. I have never heard an authoritative explanation attributing their dental health to something special in Chinese genes, or to the largely vegetarian diet, unpolished rice, minerals in the water, little sugar and no soft drinks, but something they had, or did, was exactly right.

Although chiefly from middle-class Changsha families, some of them well-to-do, the students also included members of poor families, boys who were there on scholarships from the mission schools scattered around the province. We had been for a decade the union school for a number of other missions — the Presbyterians, the Reformed Church, and English Wesleyans. The student homogeneity was emphasized by the school uniform or the alternative Boy Scout uniform; by regulation, students could wear whatever garments they wished under the uniform but not over it. Homogeneity was further emphasized by the extremely short haircuts, virtually head shaves, that suggested attachment to the Generalissimo as the model for an austere, puritanical, nationalistic leadership. Chiang Kai-shek did not usually excite adulation or demand it, but he was a cool leader with immense Face and elicited our students' support and admiration.

Since Yali's opening in 1906, its students had characteristically been involved in political turbulence and academic interruptions as they demonstrated *against* the moribund Manchu government in 1910–12 or *for* the new republicanism, or *against* the pro-Japanese, Shantung terms in the Versailles settlement of 1919, or *for* nationalist unification of China in the mid-twenties, or — in my first year — *against* the Japanese invaders. Their activism at the provincial and national levels, with its elements of antiforeignism, independence of spirit, and rejection of authority, had its counterpart on campus in student distaste for regimen and discipline within the school community. Brownell Gage, one of the founding fathers of the school and probably a rather starchy disciplinarian, seems to have borne the brunt of numerous confrontations in the early years. A bit later, in 1927, there was a student strike. In 1925 there had been widespread antiforeignism, and in 1926 even a temporary closing of the school.

Student attitudes ebb and flow, and their compulsions alter markedly from year to year. Whatever the turbulence before 1937, my era was yet a different one, one in which students seemed appreciative of Yali's existence and accepting of its reasonable and evenhanded school discipline. Representative of these attitudes were my own relations with students in class. When I entered a classroom, the class leader called out "li chen" (Attention!). The class clattered to its feet and bowed to me, the teacher, as I bowed, not quite as deferentially, in return. Since classes were generally free of discipline problems, full attention could be focused on the learning process. Routines were quiet; students stood when they recited, were low-key, good-humored, and normally polite. An occasional exception to the quiet, noticed only by an American neophyte like myself, involved the use of spittoons, one in each classroom, placed up off the floor on a framework like a high stool. There would suddenly be a rending, hawking sound as some member of the class got up, walked over to the spittoon, lifted the lid, and delivered. When chest colds were abundant, it was hard for me to pretend that these hideous sound effects were not an interruption. I now think they were given a certain dramatic caricature to poke a bit of deadpan fun at me.

I found the students not only serious and hard working but markedly adept at learning English, a feat that I regard as particularly impressive when one considers the linguistic minefields guarding the approaches of a common English verb such as "break": break up, break down, break in, break out, break out of, break off, break away, break into, break through, and so on. Part of the explanation of student skill doubtless lay in the fact that Yali students commonly felt at home in the context of multiple languages—many of them spoke not only the local Hunanese Mandarin with its five tones and provincial flavor, but at least one other dialect. In addition, they all had relentless training in memorizing poetry and vast sections of the Confucian classics. We often heard individuals walking up and down near our house, chanting ("baying" was the word) their memory work. There was a very evident carryover to their ease in memorizing English vocabulary and usable English sentences, which were promptly put to work in conversation with us.

Their linguistic adeptness helped explain their very evident dramatic skills. I would venture the proposition that a student dramatic production with quality acting could be put on faster and with less fuss in China than anywhere else in the world. Maybe a simple-minded play, with inadequate props and no lighting, but acted with flair and sophistication.

They were talkers rather than outdoorsy types. Slender, not at all muscular and only moderately interested in athletics, they seemed to stand around a lot, to kid each other, to talk and talk. Their province was reputed to have more than its fair share of tough soldiers, mean xenophobes, peppery cooks, volatile politicians, and plain women. With regard to the last, a type of head which seemed to be common in Hunan possessed a tiny nose, bright black eyes, pronounced breadth at the cheekbones, and strongly accentuated flatness of face and profile. Our students were more apt to have that central China flatness of face than the chiseled handsomeness of China's deep South. None had the large, muscular frames so often seen among the North Chinese.

I found them very likable — certainly a willing and teachable group. A group also not yet profoundly shaped by the war, not yet forced into premature choices about where to live and how far to pursue their education, choices that would have implications for their futures.

·   ·   ·

A dozen of the older students, after their own classes were over for the day, ran an informal, elementary school for neighborhood poor children. The school was entirely student-initiated and student-run. The motivation for establishing it emanated from both Christian and non-Christian boys. Two of my seniors served as principal and dean, one of them years later going on to prominence as dean of a large and important institution on Taiwan.

This elementary school, known inappropriately as the "Poor School," was located just outside one of the back gates of the campus, where it had the use of several rooms for classes and an adjacent courtyard with jungle gym for recess. Complete with regular classroom atmosphere and school routines, it offered classroom opportunities to children who otherwise would have had none.

When I photographed the Poor School, I was struck by the way my own ghost loitered in the setting. Their school mirrored in the afternoon what I had been doing in my own classroom in the morning. The

Campus moods in China were variable and cyclical. A decade before my arrival, these seniors would have been marching with placards, confronting foreigners, rejecting school discipline, cultivating turbulence. In 1937, the mood was one of purposeful education, classroom decorum, rationality, and duty. Senior high students were at that time in the uniform of military training.

relationship that I was unconsciously creating with my own students was here held up to me for scrutiny and appraisal. Fascinating to me, and a bit unnerving.

There was evident affection between the student teachers and their younger students—a phenomenon that was echoed repeatedly during my China years in the form of pleasing relations between the older and the younger, whether brothers, cousins, or friends. Distressing sibling rivalries seemed not to exist as a standard pattern. Chinese families, with their powerful pressures for hierarchical positioning of individual members, assigning them clear responsibilities and degrees of respect, seemed to have subdued, or rooted out, the blight of competing for position and affection within the family. The relaxation of certain kinds of family tensions in turn cleared the way for easy older-boy–younger-boy relations.

The Poor School students were poorly dressed but cheerful. I found

News was posted on the bulletin board just outside the chief classroom building. With minimal good news, this was inevitably a sober gathering.

Two of our Senior School students. Note big serviceable inkstone with inkstick leaning on it; pen is the traditional, fine-pointed brush, held vertically with wrist low and hand high in a manner that feels awkward for an American.

Absorbed in marbles. Note traditional cloth shoes—black, light, thin-soled, cool; and the apparent comfort of the usual sitting position with heels on the ground, body relaxed, joints loose.

More marbles. Junior School students (i.e., junior high).

Left: Volleyball, next to the chapel. This was a favorite sport, and the only one our students practiced on their own.

Right: This boy is not touching the ground. With his weight concentrated on the right pedal and his left foot hooked behind the seat, he is maintaining a precarious balance with quick, delicate adjustments of the wheel gripped in his right hand.

them as charming as imaginable, their dark eyes having the snapping brilliance so typical of young Chinese. They were stunning subjects for the prying young photographer.

.　　.　　.

John and I were phased quickly and discreetly into our jobs as English teachers. A typical senior class consisted of about fifteen students, a good size for our type of instruction which involved lots of student participation and heavy emphasis on the mechanics and ease of a working command of the language. Speaking received as much emphasis as reading, writing, grammar, and spelling combined; our generally happy results compared very favorably with my archaic instruction in German at Yale

Recess at the afternoon school for poor children. The school had simple facilities near the back gate of the Yali campus. One of our seniors (light uniform).

where my peers and I remained tongue-tied even after a fourth-year course in *Faust*.

Three classes, each meeting five times a week, were my responsibility. It was assumed that I would use the text materials chosen for me and operate within the framework of the Direct Method (i.e., I would be teaching English in English to my intermediate and advanced students, explaining grammatical points in English, and not relying on Chinese in any way in the classroom).

My I-ii class particularly could not have been easy for the students. There were forty in the section, far too many for good language work under any circumstances but especially difficult for first-year students after only one term with an instructor who could dissolve some of their frustrations by answering key questions in Chinese. The purity of the Direct Method in my classroom permitted no such luxury, although it

The children were wondrously charming.

John Runnalls in English class. In that era we would not have dreamed of going to class without tie and suitcoat.

was often diluted by clarifying chatter in Chinese from the first student to grasp what I was saying—something like a concerto where I was the solo instrument and the students the orchestra. After these initial difficulties, most of the students found their way into spoken English, many of them attaining fluency by their fifth and sixth years.

·　　·　　·

Our curriculum was bicultural in shape and emphases, and wholly at variance with the historic Chinese educational pattern of the young scholar working with a tutor on memorization of the Confucian classics, on skill in writing stereotyped essays, and on calligraphy. The main lines of Yali's modern, westernized type of education had been worked out by mission educators in the cities of eastern China during the preceding two or three generations. After the fall of the Manchu dynasty in 1912, the government of Republican China had not only accepted what the missions had pioneered, but had adopted it as a national pattern, seeking to expand, upgrade, and regulate it. By 1937, when I began teaching in

China, the general outline of Yali's curriculum was reinforced by what the government regarded as credit courses in preparation for university work. Its staples were literature, both classical and modern, history, art, and the sciences; electives, such as those offered by the Bachelors from time to time on drama, western customs, or social and economic ideas, were peripheral. From the beginning Yali's leaders and the provincial authorities of Hunan, one of China's antiforeign provinces, had observed an agreement that Yali would operate as an educational enterprise and not as a center of Christian evangelism.

In Yali's pedagogy, technique probably varied more between the Chinese and American staff than within either group. The Chinese teachers placed more emphasis on memorization and accurate repetition of what the teacher taught. We Bachelors, although our teaching of English as a foreign language was naturally captive to memorization and repetition, stood more for the ideals of arousing curiosity, getting students to ask questions, and training them to think. From the faculty and curriculum as a whole came the message that education and life in the community were closely interrelated. The Yali experience carried with it the implied obligation of making it socially useful.

The practitioner of the school's philosophy of education who was closest to us was neither Frank Hutchins, rather remote in his administrative role, nor Dwight Rugh, more involved with the special problems of the chaplaincy than with the curriculum, but Burton Rogers, the head of the English Department and architect of the type of teaching we did within it. Raised a rural New Englander in Sherman, Connecticut, he had been educated in a one-room schoolhouse, where an adroit teacher had kept interested and busy a roomful of young people, grades one through twelve, and had prepared Burton successfully for college. Upon graduation from Yale in 1930, he had first gone as a Bachelor to Yali, then done three years of graduate work in linguistics and language instruction in London and New Haven before returning to Yali as a member of the permanent staff and head of the English language program. He was friendly, capable, Anglophile in sentiment and partly in accent—both somewhat suspect in Bachelor eyes. He rode an English bicycle (then a rarity in China as well as in the States). His leadership was manifested more in departmental design than in advice or counsel—he was too shy and reserved; we, too ebullient and bursting with energy. So reserved were he and I with each other that it took us a generation to realize what good friends we were.

Burton spoke Hunanese, was able to explain points in Chinese when necessary, and could teach the difficult introductory English classes very well. He enjoyed entertaining the younger boys, and we'd hear them contentedly burbling along in a mix of English and Chinese as they sat around a table, engrossed in games with him.

In important respects he was ideal as a language instructor: he enjoyed it as a set of problems; he was normally clear in thought and presentation, precise but not frightening or condemnatory; he saw and understood the bicultural intricacies of language teaching; he made learning a foreign language seem feasible and accessible; he made it fun. He also gracefully surmounted certain hidden obstacles that we were not even acknowledging, but that are clear enough to me now — namely, language instruction's cruel imbalance between teacher and novice, a greater spread than almost anywhere else in life, too easily and inadvertently taken advantage of by an insensitive teacher. His teaching instincts were excellent, and he handled this quite complicated problem successfully and without fuss.

An admirable and efficient teacher, this modest, devoted man unconsciously exemplified what Yali stood for in education and missionary usefulness.

·   ·   ·

Teachers usually have a lopsided and limited knowledge of their pupils. At the same time, they do get insights into the talents of students as well as penetrating glimpses into bright and dark spots of their temperaments. I never knew about their times of passion, their lies and betrayals, or their moments of contempt; nor did I know their strongest yearnings, flights of imagination, or the deep rich strata of their lives. But I did have my glimpses. I was occasionally aware of how two classmates might not be on speaking terms with each other for long periods, despite the mutual awkwardness of inhabiting the same classroom month after month. There seemed to be no such thing as a fight among them, but I was given a view of a related matter near the end of my second term. I

Burton Rogers: A Connecticut Yankee in Republican China. Yale '30, member of the permanent staff, head of the English Department, the missionary as educator.

was visiting one afternoon with the proctor in his office when four tearful I-i (seventh grade) boys arrived, hesitating at the door before entering. They talked at some length with Mr. Shao, their bodies wracked with sobs. I thought they must all be guilty of some towering misdemeanor.

When they finally bowed and left, Mr. Shao explained that two of them reported having exchanged angry words, each subsequently repenting. Now each wanted to take the entire blame. The two other boys who sobbed with almost equal violence had come to ask the proctor, "Please do not punish the offenders severely, because both are sincere and good-hearted boys."

What had I witnessed? Was this an ancient traditionalism at work ("sincere" is a word of great moment in Confucianism)? Were these boys practicing an ancestral art of getting along through personal rectitude softened with compromise?

.　　.　　.

The differences between Chinese and American cultures were wonderfully stimulating, and taught me a lot about both. It had never occurred to me, for example, that there might be more than one way to enter a house, and yet a traditional Hunanese who was used to hammering on the compound gate, calling out to the gatekeeper in a voice that would have seemed peremptory or insulting to an American, and sending a servant scurrying for some member of the family, would not have known how to approach an American suburban home, ring the doorbell, ask in a normal voice for the lady of the house, take off his rubbers, hand over his coat to be hung up, enter the parlor, and be seated after the lady.

In my upside-down experience I was finding junks and wheelbarrows instead of trains and trucks; carrying-sticks instead of suitcase handles; south-pointing compasses, chopsticks, white used as the color of mourning, long fingernails symbolizing scholarship, calligraphy as an admired art form, food customarily diced and sliced by the cook's knife instead of the diner's; the rich domiciled in multiple, one-storied courtyard units; a pictographic, ideographic, nonalphabetic language which could serve as the common written medium for as many different spoken languages as existed on the European continent. Within recent memory girls' feet had been bound to assure eligibility for marriage. The dragon was a benign symbol associated with water and plentiful harvest; if St. George had sallied forth to slay one, the local populace would have lynched him. And so it went, on and on.

Many of these differences were on the surface, some simply evidence of a less developed stage in technology, as illustrated by the telephone. Although residences rarely had phones, we did have access to one over at the school buildings. Use of this involved repeated shouts to the operator, as though faintness of the signal in the wire might be compensated for by stereophonic use of the province's airwaves. These shouts typically exaggerated the five tones of Hunanese in a wonderfully clarifying way for my foreign ears, but there was waiting and waiting. Then, if the call really went through, pleased astonishment made up for the total lack of privacy of the call itself.

At a deeper level, I felt that Americans, so aware of the onrushing future, paid too little attention to the past. They stressed innovation, and sought to "save time." The Chinese, like the British, seemed to dwell on the past, happier with endless cultural repetitions than with change, and — when change became unavoidable — more at home with incremental than with radical shifts. At least, so it seemed without crystal balls in the thirties. From the perspective of the 1990s, two of the inexplicable ironies of the last two centuries seem to me to be the creating and effecting by the unlikely British and the even less-likely Chinese of such cosmic and shattering transformations as the Industrial Revolution and the Maoist Revolution. There were in each case helpful, indigenous preconditions, such as England's entrepreneurial skills from the seventeenth century on. But revolutionary changes in either Britain or China must be viewed as startlingly unexpected from the point of view of both societies' profound preference for a civilized gradualism.

In my cultural comparisons, then and now, there appears to be no credible norm. Which was really upside-down, East or West? The Chinese had a coherent civilization, accepted by an enormous population and historically dominant in a vast region. Why were they not the norm, and we in the West the deviants? It is impossible to resolve this question, although strident answers have often been put forward. The missionary traditionally had thought himself superior, the bearer of blessings. The Chinese, with a relentless memory of China's historic importance, so long sustained as to be almost genetic, simply knew he was superior — it was a fact, like the presence of nitrogen. In the nineteenth century these different mind-sets had led to maddening confrontations between foreigners and Chinese, but by our own era an accommodation had been achieved, partly because the Westerner had technological advantages which compensated for his innate barbarianism in Chinese eyes and made him a temporary peer. This circumstance of equality defused the Chinese's deep, sometimes crippling, sense of cultural superiority and enabled an often ideal working relationship to emerge. We had that at Yali.

How does one illustrate the quintessential Orient, the China that I found so different from the States? Through rice paddies? Water buffaloes? Junks? Dilapidated city walls? Scholars in long gowns? Surely through all of them. My answer here is — through a view of the main street of a provincial town, Nanyo, with typical dress, view, shop signs, a pilgrimage mountain in the background, the mountain juxtaposed to the flat valley bottom.

· · · ·

Our students had not grown up in an atmosphere of athletics. My own youth is hard to imagine without an addiction to sandlot baseball and the Boston Red Sox, perennially frustrating in that era too; without my awareness of the National Hockey League and the Boston Bruins; my commitment to tennis, lacrosse and swimming; my enjoyment in watching prep school and college athletics.

There was a struggling athletic program at Yali which consisted of intramural exposure to soccer, volleyball, basketball, and track. Although there was no athletic fanaticism American-style, and no program of playing teams from other schools, some students were well-coordinated and enjoyed participation. They were often nimble and graceful athletes, but unmuscular, skinny, and certainly not built for contact sports, which were understandably absent from the program. I taught some of them to play softball, and we had a lot of fun together, I expounding niceties like: "The base runner trying to score from second base has to go by way of third and not run directly home through the pitcher's box." My team played a spring game against the med students and did very well, losing respectably at 9–6.

In December at a key point of discouragement in the course of the war, a time when the school was shaken and in disarray, John and I introduced touch football to our youngest boys; they were enthusiastic and skillful, learning very quickly to run and dodge, and to throw good quick short passes. So captivated were they, they mentioned it as soon as I arrived in class, and again before I left; they showed up at our house during lunch to be sure they were on hand as soon as John and I were ready. Each day we played an hour, often two. John and I were still newcomers to spoken Chinese, but the students didn't hesitate much in using their classroom English, and the language barrier quickly dissolved in the frenzy of the athletic encounter. I think the students found John and me bouncy, engaging, and refreshingly different from the Chinese staff who made up most of the faculty and who were necessarily more parental, more formal and distant.

Changsha: Autumn 1937

Our Chinese friends all seemed to regard Cantonese cooking as clearly the leader of haute cuisine, yet equally good in my Changsha experience were the best Hunanese, Szechuanese, and Moslem restaurants, each with its excellent provincial specialties. A favorite Hunanese dish was pork with a thick layer of attached fat, which had been whitened and lightened by being blown full of air before being simmered in stock. Another was a whole poached fish served under a thin ginger sauce. Both of these dishes were tender enough to be plucked apart with chopsticks. Fish, chicken, and pork were all relatively abundant in Hunan, where at the slightest encouragement they would be served with pepper hot enough to open your pores. The province was famous for its political antics — like Bengal in India — and reference was often made to the interplay between pepper and hot-tempered Hunanese politicians, much as one would couple the Irish with Guinness or whiskey.

Hunanese cuisine did not aspire to the high inventiveness of Cantonese, but it derived from the same necessity of exploiting limited resources to the utmost — food taboos and squeamishness being generally disregarded. I was confronted with my fair share of chicken heads and fish eyeballs, and I heard of feasts with snakemeat delicacies and Tibetan caterpillars.

The major exception to uninhibited cooking was that milk and milk products were conspicuously absent from Chinese diet; and abhorrence 69 of cheese was unanimous. The explanation of the nonuse of milk probably lies partly in the lack of refrigeration, but chiefly in the absence from Chinese bodies, for genetic or other reasons, of certain enzymes which are necessary for the digestion of milk. Western doctors are now familiar with that condition, both among individuals and large racial and cultural groups.

When people wanted to entertain us, they commonly invited us to a restaurant, rather in the French style. Their own living quarters, which were apt to be small and to contain several generations of family members, were not suitable for congenial entertaining. Moreover the restaurants were at once excellent, not expensive, and their atmosphere was relaxed.

For a Hunan feast — the noun we invariably used for fancy dining-out — the guests drifted together at a designated restaurant at different times during the two hours before food was to be served. That was the time for conversation, not after the meal. Those who were free and wanted to visit at length came early. The indeterminate beginning gave comfortable flexibility to people with competing engagements or to those who came by foot, bicycle, boat, or rickshaw from some distance. There were no cocktails or aperitifs. The guests drank tea and ate roasted watermelon seeds as the conversation flowed.

When we sat down to the feast itself, we normally were confronted with four cold dishes, which looked inviting but which we Bachelors tried to avoid because of various fly-borne disasters which could befall us; we then had sequentially up to ten dishes which were served hot (much safer for us), one of them a sweet dish, and each greeted upon its arrival with a bottoms-up toast of hot wine in very small cups. The wines were palatable but not at all comparable in range and subtlety to Rhenish, French, or California vintages. The tables being round, each person, once armed with porcelain spoon and chopsticks, was democratically equidistant from the dishes in the center. The host, seated with his back to the door, might graciously lift choice morsels onto his guests' plates, accompanied by many protestations from the recipients over their unworthiness of such courtesy. The rice arrived only near the end of the meal, at which point the wine was removed. I think the explanation for that firm removal was not that rice and wine mixed badly, but that the festivities were approaching their end. We often topped off with sliced oranges, when they were in season, before the appearance of a tray of steaming face towels, one for each guest. The towels were followed without delay by everyone's departure. There was no dawdling and no attempt to make conversation on a full stomach. The feast was over.

·   ·   ·

With the Changsha Airport less than a mile from the school and the prevalence of heavy autumnal mists, the big Eurasia plane from Hankow often came thundering in just a few hundred feet over our heads. Eurasia was a Sino-German air transport company with three regular weekly flights from Hankow through Changsha and Canton to Hong Kong. Pan American Airways also entered our lives. In a daring innovation in 1937, Pan Am had built the China Clipper and instituted scheduled flights across the Pacific. By finishing my letters for home before a given deadline, I could get them via plane or train to Hong Kong to catch the Clipper leaving on Thursday of each week for transit to the States in a magical ten days overall, if everything went right—although it seldom did. Our mail from home sometimes required ten weeks. We found that after it had arrived briskly at Hong Kong by Clipper it was then sent on to us in Hunan by surface, like a relay with the hare handing the baton to a tortoise. We took to urging friends to add postage for air mail from Hong Kong to Changsha. That seemed to make a difference.

I used care, as the others did, in choosing a variety of stamps, and encouraged my family to do the same. Bedecked with six or eight of the most colorful stamps available, the envelopes had an impact all their own. The incoming ones were great prizes for the many avid stamp collectors at Yali. The outgoing ones were subject to certain risks what with the deepening difficulties of the war and the further circumstance that one of our servants was removing from the envelopes some of the expensive stamps and selling them. This was one of those pathetic episodes that were so trivial and yet so revealing of cultural assumptions. He had become saddled with funeral expenses, a cruel and terrible burden that we learned was commonplace, involving sums well beyond the capacity of the dutiful son to pay without severe and continuing hardship. I think that for many Chinese a real part of their sense of personal security was the assurance that they would be buried in a traditional, heavy, lacquered wooden coffin, joining their forebears in a family site, their departure expensively celebrated with priests and food and ceremonial. It was hard for an outsider to be understanding and sympathetic, since it seemed such a foolish overrun for people already on the edge of survival, but it was all tied up with the profound respect of the fading Confucian society for the family. One of the most sensitive areas of family relations remained that of the duties of the eldest son to his parents — both alive and dead.

In our case, John, in charge of the household at that time, finally got it all straightened out with minimal punishment of the offender. Among other things, we relied not only on that servant's customary loyalty but on his good cheer and sense of humor.

. . .

One of my ways of snatching relaxation was to go birding. Since Phil Greene was not only a buoyant and friendly man but had both binoculars and a strong interest in South China birds, he was an ideal companion for these forays. On campus we could observe mynahs, a species often caged by the Chinese because of their capacity to mimic words; an occasional hoopoe, with bold black and white bars on tail and wings, softly cinnamoned from head to breast, slender down-curving bill and a princely crest; a nest of magpies in the tall camphorwood tree near the chief classroom building; and, loveliest of all, nesting paradise fly-catchers — a medium-sized bird with cobalt head, crest and beak, and either snow-white or fox-red body. Two thin feathers projected about eight inches beyond the regular tail feathers. Its flight, designed to keep those fluttering feathers clear of snags, had a rounded, swooping character. Many of us were fascinated by this gorgeous bird, but none knew whether the coppery feathers of some of the fly-catchers indicated a difference in sex, age, or species from the others with the vivid, white, body feathers. In the countryside, rice paddies commonly held egrets and parson crows — the latter's black set off by a clerical collar of white. Near ponds we could see azure kingfishers, exquisite, darting flashes of blue, white, and russet. On the rivers we saw cormorants put to use by commercial fishermen. Dark-eared kites were one of the common scavengers of the region, often seen over river or harbor. Behind Phil's house we found woodcock; elsewhere, azure jays, golden-rumped swallows, Philippine red-tailed shrike, and black-naped orioles. We never enjoyed access to forest cover in the denuded hill country of Hunan. And we were never aware of wild animals — snakes, foxes, badgers, squirrels, or the like.

I was told a story of recent vintage concerning a tiger found swimming the Hsiang River. It seemed to me astounding to have a big cat in water, and, miraculous for it to be crossing such a wide river — clearly an animal and an event to be cherished in such an unlikely area as our Central Hunan. Once safely across, the tiger would have been within easy reach of a hill country virtually devoid of population, but it was harassed, pushed under, and drowned by a cruel and thoughtless boatman — the animal's defeated body later being displayed in the city. There were things about China I was sorry to learn; that story was one of them.

. . .

Linguistically isolated and culturally beleaguered, I was more dependent on friends and acquaintances than I would have been in the States. There was a lot of old-fashioned visiting, and much affable conversation at teas and parties. If someone made the effort to cross the river and walk a couple of miles to pay a call, he or she was commonly invited to dinner as well. Having servants, our entertaining was simplified, and we had more time for each other. Group forays by bus and bicycle were pleasant evidence of this. Altogether it was quicker and easier to make friends there than in the States.

Our Yale friend, Rocky Chin, after his arrival from Hong Kong in the fall of 1937 often came to call. He had found work teaching English at an officers' school over near the base of Yo-lo Shan (Mount Yolo). He knew a lot about international relations, having just taken a Ph.D. in that field at Yale and written a dissertation on the Japanese textile investment in Shanghai. A very likable, capable and unpretentious individual, thoroughly Americanized, Rocky was on an earnest identity pilgrimage, struggling with the language and trying to sort out his personal link with the complex land of his forefathers.

Jimmy Yen became a friend when he rented a house for his family near the hospital and entered his sons in Yali. A well-known YMCA secretary for Chinese labor troops in France in World War I, he had become the inspired leader of the Mass Education Movement, as well as one of the originators of the Rural Reconstruction Movement of the 1920s and 1930s. During this period of China's most intense modernization, he was being used as an advisor to the Generalissimo. Dr. Yen was in and out of Changsha a good deal, a slim winning man with a lined face and a quick smile, an idealistic yet practical statesman, humane and charming. Mrs. Yen, more highly Americanized than her husband, was regularly present in Changsha and visible in and around Yali.

George Lin was entirely different — a westernized businessman who had attended college in California, unsmiling and brusque, fluent in English, eager to make friends with the Yali Bachelors, and indeed, almost the only Chinese friend who invited us easily and regularly to his home. Sid, George Lin, and Jimmy Yen enjoyed tennis and played well, although the increasingly desperate times meant fewer opportunities.

Our fellow foreigners in Changsha — just a few dozen individuals — were inevitably a part of our social lives. Missionaries and businessmen formed two groups, not much interconnected. The Changsha mission community consisted of two or three dozen hardworking men and women, some of them Catholic, but mostly married Protestants, who were involved in running middle schools, churches, hospitals, and a school for the blind.

One of the most remarkable missionaries in Changsha was Dr. Fritz Eitel of the Liebenzeller Mission. I met him but never came to know him well, to my lasting regret. One of Burton Rogers' warm friends, a highly trained and very gifted doctor, he had had an unusually rough time as a medical pioneer in Hunan. His first hospital had been looted in 1930 by the Communists during their brief occupation of Changsha; a second hospital, located in western Hunan, was similarly looted when the Long March went through his area; his third and largest, again in Changsha, was, within a year of my meeting him, burned out in one of the war's great urban disasters (p. 233). He was a fine flute player, an excellent linguist, at once the most culturally sophisticated member of the Changsha mission community and the representative of a fundamentalist German mission affiliated with the China Inland Mission. His hospital, down in the heart of the city, possessed the province's only fluoroscope for lung scans. During a visit to Germany, the Nazis put him in jail, but he was released to go back to China where he served British and American missionaries in a Japanese internment center in North China; yet later, after residence in the postwar period near Philadelphia, he practiced for some years in Japan, where he died. A wonderful man, beloved by those who knew him.

The foreigners of the business community were very different. I was spared a full exposure to them and their expatriate, alcoholic, mercantile culture, since many had left Changsha because of the war, ending the high period of their presence in Hunan. Some remained.

Prominent among them were the BAT and APC men, i.e., representatives of the British and American Tobacco Company and Asiatic Petroleum Company, a subsidiary of Royal Dutch/Shell. Cigarettes were very widely used in China in 1937, mild and successful brands being put out in small packs of eight or ten cigarettes by BAT. As for petroleum products, the basic market over several generations had been kerosene for lamps, sold in tiny, individual portions but to a very large number of households. More recently there had developed a modest market in lubricants and fuel for railroads, steamships, gunboats, and automobiles, which were slowly penetrating Hunan.

The foreign business community seemed to my hostile eyes to be a dreary group locked into an unsavory lifestyle in cheerless frame houses on the Island, a long sandbar off Changsha in the middle of the Hsiang River. The Island gave the foreign businessmen an aloofness which was underlined in their social life at the Club, a center for cards and drinking with a membership until recently exclusively Caucasian. Their lives seemed a mindless stereotype of the blight of European imperialism anywhere from Casablanca to Shanghai.

If these individuals remained for some years in China, they tended to become caricatures of themselves. Cut off from the sanctions of family, neighborhood, and their own national cultures, they grew into ungainly, larger-than-life, foreign eccentrics, with too much money and influence, too easy alcohol and sex. Communicating in pidgin English with their Chinese servants and business associates, they seemed to my twenty-two-year-old eyes to be political reactionaries, alien and alienated, contemptuous of Chinese culture and of its weakness and problems. Their regular Western salaries, with travel allowances as well, went fantastically far in China in 1937, when a servant could be hired by a foreign businessman for a couple of American dollars a week. The servant might have to put up with insults in pidgin and with being bawled out before the other servants, but might tolerate these indignities for some time because of his salary and the opportunity for squeeze. The businessman himself could live a life of comfort and indulgence and still save against a return to his own country.

The individual who seemed the most interesting to me was a former fundamentalist missionary who had left his mission post to represent a German cartel marketing chemical dyes in central China. Fluent in Chinese, English, and German (his native tongue), and totally accommodated to a kind of bicultural lifestyle, he seemed to me a character right out of Joseph Conrad. Although wrinkled and bent when I met him, he had not so many years earlier had a son by a mistress. The child had been accepted by his wife and adopted by them.

Clearly enough, our small foreign community in Changsha had an extraordinary range of types, and it did me good to get to know them.

.　　.　　.

On a Saturday morning in late October, John and I joined Lois Greene (ear, nose, and throat specialist on our hospital staff) by shortly after seven to walk into the city to catch the public bus to Nanyo Shan, the Southern Sacred Mountain, south of Changsha and across the river. Our four hours of relatively rapid, swaying transit were interrupted at one point by a stop in the countryside. The driver dipped water from a brook and apparently poured it into the engine's carburation system. To my "Do Chinese buses run on WATER???" Lois replied: "Some, with conventional engines and a special attachment invented in 1932 by a young Changsha scientist, run on methane produced by a mixture of charcoal and water." The buses obviously ran effectively, although they had a languid acceleration.

After lunch in Nanyo at a small hotel made over from a temple, we began our exploration of the local Buddhist sites. The temples, part of a famous pilgrimage complex, had heavily proportioned roof corners,

Three exemplars of China's westernization. Left to right: Dr. James Y. C. Yen, Yale graduate, former YMCA secretary, originator of the Mass Education Movement. George Lin, University of California graduate, energetic English-speaking business-man. Joan Wang, daughter of an English mother and Chinese father, one of the early tennis players of China, National doubles champion with her sister.

lavish carvings of dragons and phoenixes, statues of Kwan Yin, the Goddess of Mercy, of the Buddha and his disciples, but the mellow bells echoed through nearly empty worship areas. The pilgrimage season of August to mid-October had been slow, we were told, because of the war; and our visit was late, anyway. We did see a few visitors who were recognizable as pilgrims because they were wearing the customary small red pilgrim bibs, tied around the neck and covering the chest.

Fewer pilgrims meant that less than the usual number of beggars had gathered in the town, but there were some. One, an apparent spastic, lying in the street, clothed in rags and covered with dust because he had to propel himself jerkily along the cobblestones, called out to us and, as we tried to step past him, reached up, seized the bottom of my coat, and laughed grotesquely and mockingly as I froze, my heart pounding with fear. Later on Lois, a doctor, got us to scrutinize a young beggar's extended hand, which seemed terribly clotted with gangrene, blood and pus. In fact, it had all been very cleverly faked with wax.

I had never had to deal with beggars before my trip to China, and I found them bewildering. How should a person of conscience, someone warmly clothed and well-fed, deal with their importunities? During a normal pilgrim season in peacetime there would have been one beggar every two hundred feet up the four thousand foot mountain — some fakers and professionals; but many of them were genuine victims of gross pathology and fearful miseries, all displayed with an Asian denial of privacy. The pious pilgrims on the Nanyo mountainside could at least control the situation because the beggars had taken up fixed stations, but in most of China's wartime cities a different situation prevailed. For example, on one of the main streets in Chungking in the summer of 1938 when I was stopped by a beggar and gave him something, I was almost instantly surrounded by thirty or forty people, pushing, pleading, and — when I withdrew into refusals — glowering and muttering. The solution that the baffled and well-intentioned foreigner was driven to accept was to be generous in support of organizations that were trying to cope with China's problems — like Yale-in-China itself — and to assume in self-defense a stance of brusque rejection of beggars on city streets. Whatever one did, one teetered between rudeness and guilt, and felt bad about it.

By the end of the afternoon at Nanyo we began our ascent of the pilgrimage trail, the weather still superb, with bits of mist collecting in the valleys. After tea at the Taoist halfway temple, where I maddeningly dropped one of our precious oranges — mine — and watched it roll out of sight down the mountain, we continued our climb in dusk and dark, reaching the Buddhist monastery near the summit by eight or so, in time for a late supper and bed in the guest quarters. Although I slept little, I felt none the worse for it, got up at six-thirty, and walked with Lois the short distance to the Taoist summit temple to watch the sunrise.

There were tall, willowy stands of pampas grass with fluffed-out, cottony heads which caught the early sun and seemed to celebrate the glory of the Buddha. These stands remain a favorite memory of autumn in South China. Back at our Buddhist monastery, we visited the kitchen before a filling breakfast of vegetables, bean curd, half-polished rice, and tea.

We watched the monks at service—chants, gongs, bells, drums, and incense; and at the ceremonial feeding of the birds before their own breakfast. Our host monk, all smiles and affability, was most attentive. He proudly exhibited a pocket knife, the gift of a previous Yali Bachelor, and consented to have his picture taken—once on his terms, all stern formality—and then on mine, wreathed in smiles.

It was of absorbing interest to me to take part in this ancient pilgrimage, to visit the grand temples of the pilgrimage establishment, to glimpse monastery rituals that had been going on for a millennium, and to witness the medieval role of monasteries as inns in remote areas, such as our four thousand foot summit, where no regular hostelries existed. Buddhism may have been in my time in a period of long-standing decline, the grand temples of Nanyo probably commercially exploitative of the pilgrims, the monastery personnel depleted and doubtless often decadent, but there was enough telling evidence of an earlier vigor and grandeur to be vastly exciting to a history enthusiast like myself. Having seen Nanyo in 1937, I now find it easy to think of the sumptuous era in T'ang China when Chinese Mahayana Buddhism, with its paradox of mysticism and state-building aspiration, prevailed over large areas of the mainland. I can visualize the many well-established study centers, temples, and monasteries, with their impressive leadership of great abbots. I can imagine the near takeover of the court and emperorship by Buddhists, and even the eventual backlash against Buddhism, complete with inquisitorial persecutions and confiscation. Nanyo is to me a fossil from that pivotal era for Buddhism in China.

We left in the sunshine at about nine in the morning and wound our way down by a different trail, stopping for tea. Leaving Lois to wait for a sedan chair, John and I—exhilarated and ultimately exhausted—ran down the five miles to the China Travel Service, unaccountably beating the chair only by the half-hour start we had on it. After a meal and trouble over our return trip, we were able to get on a bus that had no seats, a very dirty floor, and much contested *lebensraum*. Nevertheless, our return went swiftly and safely.

Main street with the pilgrimage mountain in the background.

·   ·   ·

The Changsha climate was variable. Snow was a novelty and source of joy to us, but the winter days—with Fahrenheit readings in the forties and fifties and no central heating—were numbingly cold. Sunless and wet, they were somber and depressing as well. The rainy season had begun in late October; it rained often—in fact, much of every day.

My response to the cold was to make my debut in November in a padded long-gown worn over Western shirt and trousers. Ruth Greene and I made an expedition to town on a very cold day to purchase cloth for the garment, its lining, and the washable covering. The store, with high ceilings, no central heating, and large doors open to the street, was only slightly warmer in than out. It did have some little beds of bright charcoal embers on flat, movable fireplace units. Around them, small knots of people were warming their hands and feet.

"The mellow bells echoed through nearly empty worship areas."

Our host monk

Taoist Temple at the summit at sunrise.

The store was crowded and active, with tea being served to customers, many of whom sat about talking to the relaxed salespeople. A rock garden could be seen at the rear.

Ruth and I wandered about, feeling the wonderful cottons and silks, asking prices, and chattering like housewives. The bolts were about two feet wide, and it took a piece fifteen feet in length to clothe me. When my purchase had been carefully measured, Ruth said, "Notice that the store added a foot of its own as a customary and ingratiating dividend." The garment, when complete, was expected to cost about 20 dollars Mex (i.e., $6 or $7 U.S.), three of which ($1 U.S.) covered the labor. It proved to be well tailored, although always a bit too snug at the neck and too confining at the knees — that is, better adapted to a sedentary Chinese scholar than an active and athletic American. But, most important, it was very warm.

We were at the latitude of the Mississippi delta; snow in sufficient abundance for a snowball fight was a treasured rarity.

Occasions for being with Ruth Greene, as on this particularly nice day, were to be fewer than any of us dreamed. The war soon changed all our plans. In the account of her China years — *Hsiang Ya Journal* (Archon Books, 1977) — we have a modern missionary classic dealing with the connection which she and her remarkable doctor-husband had with the Yale-in-China medical school and hospital in the 1920s to 1940s. We get insight into their motivation for going to China, the stress — particularly for the missionary's wife — of family decisions and separations in those turbulent decades, but also the growth of intimacy and trust with Chinese students and colleagues. Her story is not a grand and glossy tale of foreigners in Peking and their sleek friends in the Legation Quarter, but a loving and observant account of how a hard-working and devoted mission family pioneered Western medicine in the provinces under conditions which made extravagant demands on their resilience. Ruth herself was one of the splendors of the mission scene.

War Comes to Changsha

It was all too good to last. I was reading in midafternoon one late November day as Ann and Fritz Greene were playing ping-pong on the porch, when I heard the rumble of what sounded like bombers followed by several thuds and a noticeable jolting of the glass door. It was indeed an air raid, although the sirens followed rather than prefaced it. We could see two pairs of bombers — high and seemingly right over us, although actually over the city on our south — that soon disappeared, followed rather tardily by Chinese pursuit planes from the airfield near our campus.

At the "All Clear" we left on our bicycles to investigate. Thousands of people were streaming along the Wall Road toward the railroad and the Bible Institute. We followed along, stopping at the top of a rise, hoping to see over the crowds, but were driven back by angry soldiers. Leaving our bikes at the Bible Institute, we became separated. I set off toward the tracks and soon saw my first air-raid victim, a corpse with bloody face and left hip destroyed, covered with some coarse black cloth and paper near the brick kilns, his family in a nearby hut loud in their grief. I crossed the bridge, saw another body being carried away, and made my way to where a crowd was looking at a dud hole next to the tracks. A crater some thirty feet in diameter could be seen close to a rice warehouse. Another body lay under a cloth nearby.

John was there with T. C. Chang. We crossed the tracks together and walked to the Institute to see two more craters, discovered a solitary blackened head with the jaw blown away and, further on, scalp and hair and isolated bones with adhering flesh. John found some bloody skin, nothing else, plastered onto a brick wall. Nearby, an explosion had blown bricks about like leaves and knocked over a rickety house, distributing its tiles in waves across an adjacent roof. Taking John back to the first casualty, we found the victim's wife bowed next to her husband's body, wailing before a small fire of Buddhist "money" for the safe passage of the soul, three joss sticks stuck in the dirt near his feet, his left leg having been pushed into position and then fallen slightly askew under the covering cloth.

When we returned the next day, the exact number of bomb craters seemed to be seven, plus the one dud near the tracks and possibly another inside the rice godown (warehouse). We saw many of the traditional, heavy, wooden coffins, and learned that bombs had fallen on two small hotels crowded with refugees from Shanghai and Nanking, resulting in some hundred dead. There were survivors picking over the tangled remains of about ten smashed houses nearby. Yali boys, some of them with gauze over nose and mouth, were on guard to keep the crowd moving.

It was Thanksgiving Day, 1937. We had our youth and health and indeed much else to be thankful for. But much, also, had changed for us in the last forty-eight hours.

·   ·   ·

A frequent supper guest of ours in the spring of 1938 was Hans Borchardt, a German who was courting Edna and who had undergone professional military training in pre-Hitler and early-Hitler times in Germany. My memory is that, according to the Hitlerian racial formula, he was Jewish — that is, one of his grandparents was Jewish — and he was therefore vulnerable to persecution in Nazi Germany, but his military record was so good (and, probably, his sponsor so powerful) that the racial aspect had been overlooked up to that time. A quiet, amiable, military technician, he was part of the group of German military advisors with General von Falkenhausen, under contract to the Nationalist government in Nanking. Borchardt was an antitank expert who had

Simple affairs cut into the Hunan clay, our bomb shelters were welcome but soggy and uninviting in the wet weather of the Changsha winter.

recently been at Soochow headquarters for the Shanghai front with Falkenhausen and the Generalissimo. Although I was a pacifist and could be argumentative about it, I don't remember clashes with him. Rather, I found his conversation very agreeable and his descriptions and comments on the war immensely absorbing, especially his detailed account of the recent campaign for Shanghai.

His reading of the early days of the war was that the Japanese in the summer of 1937 had planned to work south on the rail lines from Peiping and Tientsin, taking the area north of the Yellow River and adding it to the already large mainland regions under their control from Korea through Manchukuo.

The Chinese, realizing this, put some weak divisions in front of them and sent their own crack divisions to Shanghai with the purpose of starting hostilities there so as to distract the Japanese from their plans in the north. To Borchardt, it was a war of beginners. Instead of striking where the Japanese were weakest, the Chinese selected for assault the heavily fortified warehouses and buildings of the Japanese Concession in Shanghai. Among the further oddities of the war was that there were German advisors on both sides, each group of advisors convinced that its employer, whether Chinese or Japanese, usually disregarded its advice.

Japanese troops were rushed to this new front, landing twenty miles northwest (A) of Shanghai on the shore of the Yangtze estuary, intending to march inland and cut off Nationalist access to Shanghai from the west. But the Chinese could not dislodge their enemy from this beachhead triangle. The land was difficult. So full was it of rice paddies, canals, and farm ponds, and so few the roads, that inspection of the positions by headquarters' officers was conducted in power launches on the web of waterways. The Japanese effected a second landing (B) closer to the mouth of the Whangpu, forming an arc of a front that they then began to straighten, driving the Chinese back, village by village, and canal by canal, in slow, slogging engagements.

The Chinese position of the early autumn was just north of Shanghai's foreign concessions, but it had to be given up on October 23, when we at Yali in distant Hunan were midway in our first term. The Chinese withdrew to a line along Soochow Creek inside Shanghai itself. That was

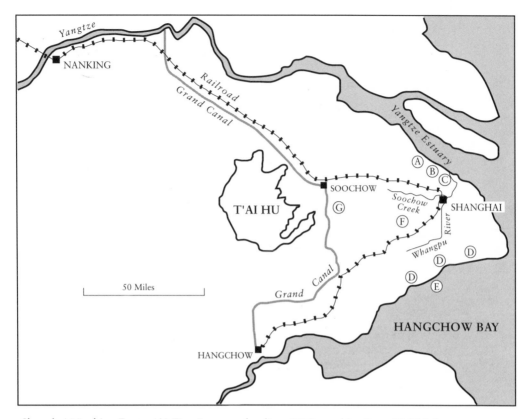

Shanghai-Nanking Front. (A) First Japanese landing; (B) Second landing; (C) Third landing; (D) Chinese divisions; (E) Japanese diversionary landing; (E to F) New Japanese position; (G) Chiang Kai-shek's headquarters.

the slowly yielding but unbroken front of November. Its southern flank on Hangchow Bay, south of Shanghai, was protected by several Chinese divisions (D).

According to Borchardt's account to me, the commander of these divisions was none other than Chang Hsueh-liang, son of a well-known warlord of Manchuria and one of the Generalissimo's 1936 captors at Sian (when the Generalissimo had been forced to shift from struggling with the Communists to confronting the Japanese). If the Borchardt version of the command is correct, it implies that the Generalissimo—upon release by his captors—was on sufficiently good terms with one of them to entrust him with a responsible command post. That would date the later placing of Chang Hsueh-liang under prolonged house arrest sometime after the collapse of the Shanghai front.

Scholars are usually startled by the Borchardt version — and unbelieving. In support of it, Borchardt was an intelligent observer who was present at the Soochow headquarters during the Japanese end-run into Hangchow Bay. The puzzle remains unsolved.

The Japanese gains had been so bitterly won and so slow in coming that one could look at it all and think of a stalemated war, a continuation of which might irreparably hurt both parties. One could, therefore, speculate about a negotiated end to it.

At that point the Japanese command, seeking to create a diversion, put ashore on the north side of Hangchow Bay a brigade (E), without artillery, which marched inland into watery countryside bristling with Nationalist divisions. To everyone's surprise, the invading brigade moved unimpeded for a dozen miles and managed to set up a position (F) about fifteen miles south of Soochow Creek. The Generalissimo's headquarters at Soochow, where Borchardt was, nearly went crazy trying to order, cajole, activate, and prod their area commander into destroying the Japanese brigade. What the Japanese intended only as a diversion, was so successful that they consolidated the new position, poured in troops, and then daringly marched them west, away from Shanghai, upsetting the Chinese plans for an orderly retreat from Soochow Creek to their "Hindenburg Line," west of Shanghai. The invaders outmarched the Chinese, causing the latter to lose a whole series of defenses to Soochow (G) and even beyond.

Nanking, capital of Nationalist China, was sufficiently far inland as to make elaborate defenses irrelevant. Rarely in its long history had it been taken by an outsider. To be sure, the Mongols had done so, but that was late thirteenth century; and the Manchus had repeated the feat, but that was in 1644. In 1842 elements of the British navy sailed up the Yangtze, menaced Nanking, extracted a treaty from the government, and sailed away.

Now, as the Japanese army approached, Nanking was overcome by panic and demoralized by the chaotic exodus of whoever had the means of flight.

The Japanese were on the outskirts by December 10 and entered the distracted city on the thirteenth. So well had their whole military endeavor gone that—we were repeatedly told—the Japanese commander rewarded his troops by releasing them from discipline for three days, during which time they bullied, raped, burned, looted and killed in one of the most discreditable episodes of the war. And much more followed.

The incredible changes within the month from the landing in Hangchow Bay to the fall of Nanking meant deepening commitments in the war, which in the long run—as we can now see—led both Nationalist defenders and Japanese invaders into a hopeless morass from which neither escaped. Japan's military success bred disaster for victor and victim alike.

The aftermath of the Rape of Nanking was vividly felt in Changsha and at Yali. Changsha, a city of 500,000, suddenly found itself swollen to something like 800,000. Unfamiliar cars and trucks filled the roads, many of them vehicles of the wealthy who had managed to escape from Nanking.

I attended a special meeting of the school that was held the evening of December 13 in the chapel right after study hall. The chapel became as noisy as a zoo until Principal Lao entered with one of the VI-i boys. The latter was about to leave for aviation school and was given an ovation. Mr. Lao broke the news to us of one of the exceedingly inflammatory international incidents of that period, the bombing by Japanese planes of the American gunboat *Panay* on the Yangtze near Nanking. He also announced the Minister of Education's decision to close the Upper School on the following Saturday after some examinations, its students to undergo a form of military training; the Lower School, he said, would continue in operation.

In the midst of these aspects and pressures of the war, and with the manifest threat now of a Japanese invasion of Central China, parents were withdrawing their children from the school. I recall how one of my classes—normally thirty-five—had ten students on the Monday after Nanking; four on Tuesday; three on Wednesday; one on Thursday; and none on Friday. The Lower School dwindled dramatically from over two hundred to a skeleton of forty-nine who finished the term in the last week of January 1938. Despite these reduced numbers, a beginning of the second term was contemplated for February 18. It was in those dog days of December that John and I introduced touch football (spoken of elsewhere) to cheer up our younger students.

In December there were many other evidences of the war, even in our interior province. In midmonth we were particularly aware of Yunnan soldiers, thousands of them, who had walked for two months from the southwest, and were pausing in Changsha, before going on eastward later in the month. Contrary to the standard reputation of provincial soldiers, they were cheerful, well-mannered, and well-disciplined. Their French rifles and warm uniforms were different from those of the many bedraggled recruits whom we observed in Changsha being drilled with closed umbrellas, hoping to inherit a precious rifle at some later point. There were by this time sixty small bomb shelters which had been dug on the campus, the persistent bad weather of midwinter also giving us protection against air raids. We were much aware of the increase of railroad activity, with the station about a mile away and the Hangchow-Canton mainline passing the end of our road, just to the east, where about half-a-dozen sidings had been added for a makeup yard and where action went on day and night, as the train whistles attested.

With a smaller school and a less distant war, the first evacuation of our personnel took place. Dwight Rugh left with Winifred, his wife, and Betty Jean, then less than five years old, on December 24. He was to be on the staff of the YMCA in Honolulu for the rest of the school year. Protestant missionary families in twentieth-century China learned to be extraordinarily adaptable; every member of the family had to be able to cope with difficult family dilemmas and separations. It was thought likely that Dwight, after getting his family settled somewhere in the States, would return to Yali for the next school year.

The departure of the Rughs took place on the first international train, together with many other foreign families from various parts of Central China to our north. The American State Department was urging speedy evacuation. Then, on Thursday evening, December 30, 1937, John and I returned from the railroad station, our hearts just about broken. The happy early phase of our China year was clearly over. We had just witnessed the departure of the second international train for Hongkong, and on it Sid, Chat, the whole Kuling American School from northeast of us, Ruth Greene and the four Greene children, and many other friends. The excitement of the evacuation maintained our morale until departure. The station had been alive with voluble speakers of English, German, and Chinese; there were British sailors, Chinese police, soldiers with fixed bayonets, baggage strewn about, large foreign flags atop the cars, passengers packed into the very limited space of corridors and compartments, everyone tense and animated, bustling about, bidding adieu, the rain falling, and mud underfoot. Ruth later wrote that the train trip had been safely accomplished in thirty-six hours, but from Canton on they saw evidence of fearful bombing, shattered villages, and people pitifully raking at the wreckage of their homes. Not long after arrival Ruth learned how a following train had been derailed, with sixty lives lost. She somehow coped with the refugee glut of Hong Kong, and her own acute puzzlement over where to go — and got her children down to the Philippines.

For us this whole aftermath of the fall of Nanking was depressing. In case the Japanese now captured Nanchang or Hangchow — the one southwest, the other southeast, of Nanking — Yali would move to western Hunan to a site already selected. I could hardly grasp how our lives could have changed so much in two weeks.

. . .

We adapted as well as we did partly because we were busy, with little time for self-absorption, but also because we were in a context where everyone around us had to adjust and adapt and carry on, a very stabilizing element in a chaotic situation. In that period the story of Dr. Jeannette Lin, a new acquaintance from eastern China, not only represented that of countless middle-class refugees, but illustrated the type of response which buoyed and strengthened those around her.

A product of westernized middle school education in Shanghai, Dr. Lin had taken her medical degree at Peiping Union Medical College (PUMC), the elite medical school of China, entered practice in gynecology and obstetrics in Soochow in the mid-1930s, and built up a small hospital.

At the time of the collapse of the Shanghai front in the fall of 1937 she had been down with the flu, but managed to get away from Soochow

93

Left: Yunnan soldier en route to the then-distant front, with enough shoes to get him there.

Below: Some Yali students did volunteer work with the soldiers from Yunnan. This student is changing a dressing.

Yunnan soldier with rice thatch for rain cape and camouflage.

Dr. Jeannette Lin, gynecologist

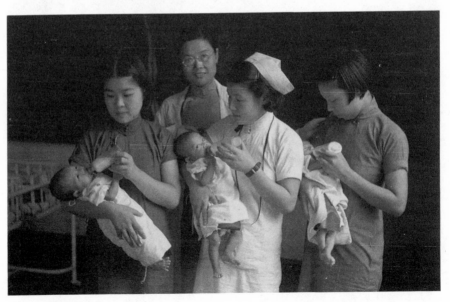

Jeannette Lin's clinic

A worried looking foundling with Dr. Lin.

Dr. Lin and the personnel of her refugee clinic, Changsha, winter of 1937–38. They had clung together in their refugeeing moves from Soochow to Nanking to Changsha. During the war at least two more moves were in store for them.

with her hospital colleagues a day or two before the Japanese took the city; she went, partly by coal boat, to Nanking, which she was shortly forced to abandon, avoiding by just under three weeks the seizure and rape of that city. She had with her the staff and some of the servants of her clinic and half a dozen infants then in her care. They came to the relative safety of Changsha, where I first met her when I photographed her tiny refugee clinic in September 1938. The babies, orphaned and abandoned in the confusion of the war, had been given a God-sent reprieve by falling under the care of these women. The nurses were young, well trained, and amiable. There was a second obstetrician, Dr. Shen Yu-ming, young, self-deprecatory, and pretty. Together the doctors established temporary housing not far from the Yali campus.

One of the special problems the doctors had was language. They not only practiced an alien, untraditional and not wholly accepted set of Western therapies, which often required explanation to patients, but they were themselves refugees from a different language zone. Moreover, they had a jumble of patients, some of them refugees too, who spoke a variety of dialects. Uneasy over my own falterings as a linguist, I especially admired these relaxed speakers of multiple tongues. Dr. Shen, the last person in the world to regard her own skills as noteworthy, spoke the Gin Hwa dialect of eastern China like a native; and she also spoke good Hangchow, Shanghai, and Mandarin, as well as some Cantonese, and some Ningpo and Changsha dialects. Her schoolgirl English, delivered slowly and blushingly, was usually accurate. Dr. Lin, a person of great animation and charm, was fully accomplished in Hakka, Shanghai, and Peiping Mandarin. She too was fluent in English, and had partial command of several dialects. Their joint skills enabled them to deal sensitively with a wide range of local and refugee patients. Who would not have found them an inspiration?

Changsha: Early 1938

The term dragged along on a curtailed basis in the clammy grayness of winter, and somehow ended in January '38. For those Chinese not dislocated and demoralized by the war, the week of Chinese New Year was a time for looking inward to the family, for pleasant calls on friends, for food and firecrackers. Also the time of year when the foreigner most acutely felt his foreignness. John and I opted to spend a week in Kweilin, capital of Kwangsi province. Southwest of Changsha, Kweilin had been the southern capital of the Ming dynasty and one of the scenic marvels of South China.

The Oriental Hotel proved comfortable, clean and so noisy with New Year's frivolity that we scarcely slept. Since meals were served only at 10:00 a.m. and 5:00 p.m., Kwangsi style, the lateness of breakfast was a problem, and we decided to move to the somewhat westernized Club. As the result of a lucky encounter with Father Glass of the Maryknoll Mission, we were invited to breakfast where we were joined by colleagues, Fathers Green, Romaniello, and Kelin, all of them football fanatics. Among us we were able to reconstruct the last football season, and spent most of the morning in continuous anecdotes on it and others past.

Late in the morning we climbed the Old Man, one of the tower-like Kweilin hills. Just outside the city wall and some five hundred feet high, the hill was one of hundreds of small mountains shaped like chicken croquettes which seemed to leap from the surrounding agricultural flatness — all of them gray, often uncompromisingly steep, eroded so roughly as to cut a climber's hands, of variable height up to a thousand feet, and riddled with caves. One cave that we visited underlay two or three hills, winding and twisting past dull, rough stalactites for half-an-hour's walk. Many of those hills, with pillboxes on them, were out of bounds to us; ours was accessible, although it involved a tricky climb with a beckoning, death-dealing drop of several hundred feet.

Below us and much smaller than Changsha, the city was generally confined within its ancient wall. We could see the lattice of newly widened streets and were later told that the provincial government, autocratically intent on modernizing the city, forced people with homes in the way of progress to tear down their own houses without compensation. Rail connections with Hengyang and Haiphong, optimistically planned for completion within the new year, were expected to enhance the tourist trade and enable the province to exploit its mineral resources. Optimism seemed to flourish despite the war, still relatively distant in South China.

The optimism did not prevent the city's leadership from being very air raid conscious with exact and efficient preparations for the speedy evacuation of nearly all inhabitants to assigned bomb shelters, the hundreds of limestone caves inside and outside the walls. For fire control, large tubs of water and sand were required of all houses and shops. Mock air raids had been held for practice — a skeleton force of citizens remaining in the city to prevent looting.

Our inexperience prevented us from anticipating the degree to which a city shuts down for the first week of the New Year. Restaurants and shops were closed, our Club served no dinner even to its own guests on the eve of the New Year, and we were lucky to find a shop with oranges, cookies, and wine, with which we had the drabbest, most dispirited New Year's Eve supper on record.

We were up at 7:00 a.m. to walk about among the firecrackers which had been going off continuously since the early hours. Going out the West Gate, we passed some soldiers who, to our great discomfort, were fooling with a revolver, firing it cowboy style into the air and off toward the hills. Walking around to the South Gate, we came across the corpse of a beggar, stiff and cold and miserably alone on a bit of straw. Anyone who died at New Year's was lucky even to be noticed. We would have felt about as cheerless as the corpse at our feet had it not been for our friendly encounter with the Maryknoll fathers.

At first we had bad luck with the weather. The rainy season produced relentless cold and overcast with almost continual light rain and penetrating dampness. When the weather finally improved, Fathers Green and Glass very kindly came by to take us on an outing. We crossed the curved pontoon bridge of dozens of side-by-side sampans, walked toward the covered Flower Bridge, and stopped to watch several little boys holding long sticks of firecrackers at arm's length, blissfully letting them go off all over themselves. A man, bending over, imperturbably picked up something as two big crackers went off under his backside and a pair of dogs barked excitedly. The scene was as Chinese as chopsticks. We walked out past the Seven Stars Caves toward Mount Royal and the first of the Ming tombs. There were forty-eight of them, each tomb under a mound, each tomb totally neglected. Parallel lines of old stone figures — horses, lions, serpent columns, and statues — guarded the approach to each tomb.

The weather held, and we took pictures, nearly all of which were failures — perhaps rightly so, because we were impious egalitarians straddling the stone animals that commemorated members of the imperial family of the southern Ming dynasty. Four hundred years earlier we would have been strangled for such reckless behavior.

We walked hard on the return, setting a mission record of an hour and five minutes. Our reward was a heart-warming American meal, topped off with gingerbread and pumelo. We greatly enjoyed those gracious Fathers, both of whom were to have prolonged traumatic experiences about a decade after our visit, when the Communists took over their city.

The Catholics brought us luck, and our social life took a distinct upward turn. We met an unusual assortment of foreigners in the city. One German, tall and heavy and hard-looking, who might have stepped out of a *New Masses* cartoon of a munitions maker, dropped in at our hotel and invited us to dinner. One of his guests was a Swiss arms agent engaged in setting up antiaircraft guns, many of them on those grey limestone hilltops. Another, a lively Magyar from Canton, had a droll way of telling half of each story with his hands. Our meal was enhanced by a Chekiang wine, served cold, our first good Chinese wine. Our host had some fine apples, an incredible rarity then in interior China, and insisted that John and I each eat two. He also had fine bronzes and some handsome books on porcelains and bronzes, among them a catalogue of the recent Burlington House Exhibition in London. These volumes were especially exciting because it was close to impossible to see good collections in wartime China, and vastly easier to sample at second hand China's great works of art in the museums of Japan, Europe, and the United States.

We met two French aviators who, caught by bad weather, had managed to avoid bumpy burial grounds, rice paddies, and the omnipresent limestone hills, in a lucky search for one of the few local roads, where they had landed close to a line of telephone poles. Some American aviators also stopped at the Club, one the ex-pilot for the Generalissimo.

Professor Shrei of Kwangsi University invited us to luncheon in his home near North Gate, where we had a delightful visit with a Professor Lin, who had studied at the Yale Graduate School, 1916 to 1918, and was currently in the Foreign Office of the Nationalist government. We had a good meal which included the novelty of a fried sweet dish and individual rice-fed chickens spread-eagled over piles of rice. Summoning my courage, I had a taste of the brain and ate the head. We had a fine time and talked long. Professor Shrei presented John and me with some of the red beans of Kwangsi. Hard, rare, and decorative, they appear on a certain plant, we were told, only after it has grown for forty years, and are regarded as love and friendship ornaments in jewelry.

Another German, an expatriate doctor, called for us at the Club and escorted us in the rain to his home, where we were treated to a meal featuring chicken cooked in paper jackets, a Kwangsi specialty. The wine, mixed by our Rheinlander host, consisted of three parts strong sweet wine, one part of what he called bitter strong wine, some water, and ten drops of bitters. Served warm, Chinese style, it gave a golden glow to his flowing monologue on such topics as Chinese medicine, Chinese generals whom he took care of, prostitution, and the continuing incidence of slavery.

We met members of the Anglican Mission and a feisty Baptist, whose mission compound had been requisitioned by the university, an act which hadn't improved his disposition. He was generous with his time in showing us about, but he seemed oddly out-of-place — an impression which he confirmed by describing trips for evangelism into the Kwangsi tribal country of the Miao, where he would walk to a village, play his mouth organ to attract an audience, and then harangue them on the threat of hell-fire and the blessings of Christianity. His cocky, cultural bossiness seemed to validate all the criticisms of the stereotyped, old-style, Christian missionary.

Another day we walked to the Seven Stars Caves with their exotic, knobby, wart-like stalactites and stalagmites, dramatic in the spaciousness of those underground suites, later extensively used as air-raid shelters. Climbing one of the Seven Stars Hills, we were presented with a magnificent view, the ultimate reward of a trip to Kweilin. Mathematically exact vegetable fields covered the foreground, next the black, low house tops on the near side of the river, then the meandering river and its branches, all a bit high from the recent rain; and behind the river the black city backed by a Druid's gathering of abrupt, fantastic, limestone hills.

We couldn't resist those incredible hills, and on a later date tried another, near our first climb up the Old Man. We chose our route badly, the climbing was treacherous and led to an apparent dead end, with the usual verticality below. John, discovering handholds and footholds, got up in good style, while I fretted and struggled. At one point, unable to suppress the desire, I looked down, and that alluring glimpse nearly wiped me out. The climb involved placing my feet on a narrow ledge, holding onto a jagged knife-edged rock, and springing full length up and against the rock face, hoping to grasp a yet higher ledge with my right hand. If I managed that much, I could then work my way up. I made three springs and slipbacks; each time I could scarcely quiet my trembling knees. On the fourth I caught my hold and joined John on the peak, both of us much relieved. We found the opposite side even worse, with its direct drop of several hundred feet to a quick death. The summit gave us a glorious vista beginning with the hills on our side of the river, unob-

The Kweilin area is saturated with small gray limestone mountains. (1938 postcard; photographer unknown.)

Those tiny mountains "often uncompromisingly steep, eroded so roughly as to cut a climber's hands, of variable height up to a thousand feet, and riddled with caves." (1938 postcard; photographer unknown.)

My climber's trauma occurred on such a hill as this.

scured by mist, complete in detail; thence across the river and back toward the horizon through mist and sequential shadings of exquisite flat grays.

We clambered down a less dangerous route as daylight slipped away and made our way to the nearest steps over the city wall. Challenged in the dusk by sentries who could be heard snapping the bolts of their rifles, we hiked half a mile to a similar flight of stairs, walked up and over unchallenged, climbed the fence into the Baptist compound, and were soon on our way back to the Club. The Kweilin sentry system would hardly have kept the Greeks out of Troy, but I think the symbolism of Chinese city walls may be much more important than their effectiveness—a quixotic twist defying the Chinese commitment to practicality.

On our return trip we took a bus to Hengyang, and by the narrowest of margins caught a train for Changsha from the railroad station which was bombed just a couple of days later. Our trip back was calm except for the football rush at the Changsha station, we trying to get out of the car while several hundred people struggled to get in. Confucian decorum belonged to cobblestone streets and latticed courtyards; on the railroad it went down the drain.

We found that a girl had been born to Frank and Louise Hutchins, an act of thoughtfulness on their part which netted me $5.00 Gold from the absent Sid, who had bet on a boy. Also, an air raid had preceded us by a day, breaking windows in Mr. Lao's house but otherwise not causing damage on the campus.

A week later another raid took place, the third for Changsha. John and I heard the rumble of the planes, ran for the door to see them, heard the antiaircraft boom and pop, thought better of it, and rushed back to prostrate ourselves on the Peiping rugs in the living room as the floor and windows shook. The only Yali casualty was our dignity. The raid proved to be on the airport. Phil later told us that one of the four fatalities was brought to the hospital, with hands and wrists blown loose, some six inches of brain laid bare, and was still able to talk to the doctor before dying.

On the cheerful side, with the invasion of Central China apparently not imminent, Yali reopened with over three hundred students, six times the number which had finished the first term.

* * *

One of the luckiest things that happened to me in China was my friendship with the German Jewish refugee, Dr. Walter Liebenthal, Sanskrit scholar and Buddhist savant. Although a learned linguist, he needed help with written English and asked for my assistance. In the winter, he and I worked repeatedly at his translation of the Book of Chao, a sixth century work of devotion and theology that he regarded as one of the key documents in both Buddhism's overland transmission from India to China and its evolution from the hair-splitting definitions and terminology of the Hinayana into China's more mystical and more abstruse Mahayana. In the fourth book, on which we concentrated our time and energy, the author's presentation relied heavily on paradoxes and metaphors as he endeavored to prove Nirvana to be beyond designation, without name or definition. With the manuscript nearly complete, Dr. Liebenthal spent many days at our house pecking away at the typewriter and mulling over pages which covered the round table like drifted snow.

No longer teaching German at the military school, he also lost his classes at the YMCA. Moreover, the government put a fifty percent tax on teachers' salaries at Hunan University where he had a very part-time position, with the result that his income was down to $30 Mex a month (about $7 U.S. at that time). He found that he could survive on even that by eating at the university, where board was only $10 Mex a month. He was of course unable to send any money to either the son who was then a student in Peiping or the rest of his family who were still in Germany. His spirits were remarkably good for someone in such straitened circumstances.

Troubles did not come singly to that learned and sweet-tempered man. In early April twenty-seven planes bombed the university campus in an attempt to catch the visiting Generalissimo. Dr. Liebenthal managed to get back into the hills and was not himself injured, but destruction of the university library included the single manuscript of our translation of that fourth book of the *Book of Chao*. Our work would have to be redone.

Shortly after that we had a pleasanter occasion. He was visiting at Yali when a marvellous full moon led us to expect an air raid. The First Alarm blew at bedtime, around eleven. Opening all our windows as a precaution against both flying glass and concussion damage to the precious glass itself, we took chairs out onto the lawn to enjoy the moon until the planes might come. After we had sat and talked for quite a while, Dr. Liebenthal thought of some Europeanstyle bread and a German spread of lard and onions that he had. These were appreciatively consumed in the moonlight as we enjoyed one of our most delightful hours of the spring. No planes came, and at the All Clear we went to bed.

On another occasion when we began to talk over our work he told me about Mr. Lin, one of the Russian teachers at the military school, a Siberian Chinese who was married to a Russian, both of them very rugged, primitive, disagreeable types. They formerly lived in one end of a small Buddhist temple, Dr. Liebenthal with a servant at the other end, and a monk in a room in between. Lin's child took to mocking the devotion of the monk, a man of about seventy. Antagonism grew as the Lins joined their son in a relentless, obstinate mimicry. Soon the father and mother were hammering on the wall with sticks. The monk became so upset over the Lins' special blend of profanity and malicious harassment that he hanged himself. Dr. Liebenthal, to preserve his own sanity, moved to a nearby monastery.

The simplicity and groping truth of his delivery, astonishingly detached and free of rancor, gave the account a dreadful force. My life was markedly enriched by my contacts with Dr. Liebenthal.

· · ·

I went with Tze Chen, a Yali pupil, and two of his friends to Pinhsiang by train, leaving Changsha at 8 p.m. on a Saturday evening near the end of March. Our destination was Anyuan, to visit the largest coalworks remaining in Chinese hands. The four other big ones, all in the north, had been taken over by the Japanese. After a noisy night in third class with six passengers to a compartment, people coming in and out, the door slamming, the train stopping and starting, we descended onto a darkened platform at Pinhsiang at 4 a.m. — too early to begin our walk to Anyuan. Standing around in the darkness we watched a fireman shovel glowing coals out of the firebox of an engine, and then drifted over to a small inn to wait out the last hours before daylight. The boys thought it better not to try the beds of that dispirited little hotel for such

Dr. Walter Liebenthal, Sanskrit scholar, Buddhist savant, refugee from Nazi Germany.

a short time, as well as for fear of the insect life we might find there. A shortage of chairs in the lobby condemned us to taking turns standing up and sitting down, but we drank tea, and slept head-on-arms-on-table fashion.

The day finally began to stir, heralded by a large and very vocal pig which was about to be slaughtered in front of an adjacent shop. We went out and watched the frenzied struggles, the knifing, the gush of blood, the last cries and twitches. In the absence of refrigeration, animals were customarily butchered at dawn, and the meat sold in the morning.

As soon as Pinhsiang's gates were unlocked, we set out for Anyuan, our walk taking us five miles through tranquil farmland, some of it very beautiful in the early light. We had breakfast with Tze Chen's uncle, Mr. Wang, manager of the mine, and then began the first of our inspections, a surface mine on the top of a small mountain.

The working conditions were astounding. At the pit itself boys who, unconvincingly, were supposed to be twelve years of age were pushing loads of at least a couple of hundred pounds. From them, men brought the coal down the mountain in wheelbarrows four miles on a steep, tortuous, rutty, dirt path to the railroad. One man could make two or at most three trips a day and receive $3 Mex a ton. Work was impossible in poor weather, about one hundred days in the year in that area. We picked red azaleas at the side of the path as the passing, ungreased wheelbarrows shrieked the agony of the workers.

We returned for luncheon and an afternoon inspection of the surface plant where the coal was washed, sorted, and some of it made into coke. The evening was devoted to conversation and to their learning from me, with a seedy deck of cards, how to play rummy. The Honored Guest, I was put that night in a high-ceilinged room, spartan but comfortable, that had been furnished against the contingency of a visit of inspection by Chiang Kai-shek.

Breakfast on Monday consisted of rice-and-rice-water and a plate of fried eggs, six of them, all for me, to be eaten with chopsticks. Each of the others ate his six eggs with no difficulty, I alone was driven to the indignity of using one of the porcelain spoons.

In miner's togs we rode coal cars some three miles into the heart of the mountain, where, each carrying a light, we walked through tunnels to various working faces. I found it nerve-wracking to pass timber supports that were badly split, some of them shattered, by the pressure of the mountain overhead. The miners, many of them young boys working naked in the warm temperature of the mine, earned 44 cents Mex for a twelve-hour day—in U.S. money about 10 cents at that time.

Back at the surface, we spent some time culling slag for fossils from the Jurassic, finding only poor ones. Late in the afternoon, Tze Chen and I, accompanied by a servant, walked back to Pinhsiang, stopping at a hotel overnight. When the scheduled 7 a.m. train on Tuesday was late, we climbed a nearby hill and visited some temples, returning at 10 a.m. to be told that the train might go at 12:30. A chance encounter with two ex-Yali students involved us in a luncheon at their house, with the result that when we returned to the station at 1:30 p.m. we found the train had come and gone at 1. None was expected before the following morning at 7, which would cut me out of a day of classes. It took an hour of phone time to convey this embarrassing information to Frank Hutchins in the Yali office.

The next day we were up at 6, ate eggs and gruel, and reached the station a few minutes after 7, only to find that the train which had been six hours late the day before, had already come and gone with maddening promptness. Oscar Wilde's dictum about punctuality being the thief of time had never been more apposite, but it wasn't strong enough. Punctuality seemed outrageous and inexcusable.

Tze Chen, who was not going back to Yali with me, got me onto a troop train to Chuchou where, with luck, I could catch a train for Changsha — and avoid a second, and yet more embarrassing, phone call to Frank. Very hot and slow, with pauses at every siding for trains to pass, the trip took six hours for sixty miles. Nevertheless, I made good connections at Chuchou and found tea and rice on the train to fortify the inner man for the two hour transit to Changsha. Sitting on the platform at the end of one of the cars, dangling my legs over the side, I watched the evening scenery unfold. In the hot spell during just the few days of my absence the grass had become greener and the leaves had come out. How pleasant it was to see in the paddies the first of the returned egrets.

.   .   .

On the outskirts of Changsha in an area that was being developed for a municipal project, there were tombs from Han times and the subsequent Six Dynasties — simple brick vaults which had been constructed at, or just slightly above, ground level and then mounded over with earth. Most of these tumuli had been opened and robbed, their contents long since lost or occasionally surfacing in the city's curio shops. The Changsha area had apparently been one of the principal centers for the manufacture of various bronzes, among them mirrors of the hundred-nipple type. One could also find very good porcelaneous stoneware, some of it with olive green glaze, and gray pottery figurines painted in white and red. Interesting as some of these items were, their usefulness to the archeologist had been generally eliminated by their removal from the tombs without professional examination of the tombs when first opened and without systematic dating.

Dr. Liebenthal and I walked out one day to see what was left of the tombs before further desecration of the area. We found several clustered in what must once have been aristocratic or royal burial ground, each tomb a mound some thirty or forty feet high. The corpse, surrounded by weapons, bronzes, and various treasured items, had been placed in an arched brick chamber about the size of a small bedroom, which had been closed and then carefully mounded over with the well-leached reddish clay soil of Hunan, the whole presenting the profile of an upended, boiled potato.

Since my era in Changsha archeologists have found and opened the very remarkable and very different Ch'u tombs, located below the surface at a depth approaching thirty feet, their wooden chambers near or below the water table but effectively sealed against Changsha's persistent moisture for millennia with layers of charcoal and white clay.

The Kingdom of Ch'u had flourished in the fifth and fourth centuries B.C., during the latter part of the Chou dynasty, when China was filled with hundreds of local, princely sovereignties. Ch'u having ruled this region from capitals north of Hunan, was absorbed in 222 B.C. by Ch'in, the dynastic predecessor of the great Han dynasty. One of the best known of the kingdom's literary works, the *Ch'u-tz'u (Songs of the South)*, was written by Chü Yüan. A statesman, renowned for his incorruptibility and for his early suicide, Chü Yüan was widely commemorated in the annual Dragon Boat Festival. Although the Ch'u heartland was probably in Hupei province to our north, the Hsiang River valley and the Changsha area itself have divulged the richest finds relating to Ch'u culture. In the Ch'u tombs diverse bronzes have been found—chariot hubcaps, halberds, ritual vessels, scales and scoops, mirrors with interlaced dragons or stylized birds, and swords with inlaid inscriptions. These Ch'u bronzes were the technical equals of China's best, and therefore of the world's best. Also discovered in the Ch'u tombs were wooden combs, silver seals, jade pendants, and sword sheath ornaments, along with lyres, zithers, bells, drums, and even textiles, which had been miraculously preserved in that damp climate for well over two thousand years. Perhaps most exciting of all to the art historian have been slim cylindrical wooden statues of stiffly-posed men and women. These, combined with examples from other sites, have pushed back by nearly a thousand years our dating of Chinese wood sculpture.

Given these recently discovered items, one is tempted to fantasize about the state of Ch'u for the century after Confucius, thinking of it as a well-to-do kingdom, blessed with water for both irrigation and transportation, good agriculture on the valley's red-clay flatness, a prominent walled town at Changsha, dominated by an elite which went in for music, attractive ornaments, and bronze weapons. The round, slightly convex, metal mirrors, prized and mysterious collectors' items for centuries, tell us of bronze-age artisans who were wonderfully skilled at the intricacies of smelting and casting. A civilized human presence in that general area for so long is hard for an American to grasp.

.   .   .

School work during that second semester of my first year—spring 1938—was demanding. With two members of the Yali English Department sent home when our student body had evaporated in the winter, and now with the renewed student population of three hundred for the new term, Burton, John, and I added Sid's and Chat's classes, often large, to our own.

I found myself teaching four (later five) classes, one of them at the medical school, each meeting five times a week, and with the usual hidden extras of class preparation, five hours of student conferences at the medical school, sets of papers, and service as baseball instructor and part-time lifeguard in the athletic program. Thursday was my heaviest day: two classes and two hours of conferences with medical students in the morning; two afternoon classes, athletics class (baseball) 4:30 to 6:30; supper and then an hour and a half of med school conferences in the evening. I was getting to bed soon after work ended, by 9:30 or 10:00, so that I could get up at 6:30, breakfast at 7:00, and have the freshest hour of the day for reading poetry.

John and Burton had similar programs, all entirely reasonable under the straitened circumstances of the war, all willingly undertaken by each

Dr. Liebenthal gives scale to one of Changsha's ancient tombs. The brickwork arch employed in this princely cave of the Han dynasty two thousand years ago, although common in Han tombs, was rarely used in regular Chinese architecture.

of us, and yet there remained hardly any time to get away from our work, scant recreation or social life, increasing exhaustion, and little laughter.

In that context I ran afoul of *Face* — Chinese hypersensitivity over personal and family dignity — in my largest class, really two sections that had been made into one, placing fifty-four intermediate students together. What would have been permissible, normal noises from an average class of twenty fidgety boys quickly made life impossible when fifty-

This Han tomb was one of a pair within the same grave mound. It had been taken over in 1937 by a destitute elderly couple who had rigged up primitive living quarters for themselves in the burial chamber.

four were involved. There seemed no alternative to my running a taut ship, insisting on abnormal quiet. It was hard on all but not impossible, until I discovered ten students — including the class president who was also the school's best soccer player — flagrantly cheating on an examination.

Feeling outraged and betrayed, I took their papers, crumpled them up, threw them in the wastebasket, and told the boys to leave the room. It was an electrifying scene, much too blunt and devastating for their inbred jumpiness in matters of Face. My American style of confrontation was as alien to a classroom of Chinese students, as the intensity of their commitment to Face was alien to me. While no one, in my experience, has ever satisfactorily illuminated the dark labyrinth of Face, I later came to think that it was really about *family*. It seemed tied, to a mystifying degree, to the group rather than to the individual. Moreover, *family* wasn't just the visible family, but family ramified into a fourth dimension of ancestors and descendants. It seemed related, also, to emphasis on *Li*—the decorum and etiquette of the Confucian gentleman. And *that* may have been importantly related to achieving civic harmony, for a large society, by endless softening compromises.

The situation which the students' dishonesty had created indeed required some firm action from me. I was in for a very sticky aftermath, no matter what steps I took, but I should have used more finesse than my inexperience and exhaustion permitted. I should not have crumpled the exams before the class, but segregated their examination papers and asked the proctor for help in making totally clear to the group of ten that what they had done should never be repeated. Mr. Shao, the school proctor, took over the ticklish problem that the students and I had jointly created. Acutely embarrassed by my actions, he nevertheless loyally backed me up and disciplined the students, who were also later allowed to take a make-up exam, which most of them flunked. I didn't know then, nor have I ever been shown, whether there was an accepted manner of restoring Face after a loss of it. Is there perhaps some unacknowledged mechanism for retrieving friendship through the adroit use of a mediator and an agreed-upon accommodation?

My hope to be relieved of the class, which now hated me for my crass assault on their classmates, was dashed. Although I had to teach all fifty-four, Burton did juggle the class into two sections, which helped, although it added five new hours to my schedule. One of my private crucifixions that spring was having to walk ten times a week into those sections, one of them more persistently hostile than the other. I decided to erode the coldness, which bordered on insolence, by being relentlessly friendly, by avoiding confrontations, and by being just as useful and effective as possible in my role as their English teacher. The outcome of the struggle was still unclear at the end of that exhausting term.

Changsha: Early 1938

Ironically, the chief item of my spring reading was *Crime and Punishment*.

. . .

Our friend Borchardt, the German antitank expert employed by the Nationalist government, was gloomy in May about the front north of Nanking, inferring that it might break open at any time, by saying that you couldn't make plans for anything more than two or three weeks ahead. He claimed no one had any idea how far the Chinese would retreat once they were on the run. After the undermining of Shanghai they had overretreated two or three, strong, modern and well-equipped lines of defense, thereby opening the way to Nanking, something that no one had expected.

A Chinese army of 600,000 in the vicinity of Soochow was, within three days of my conversation with Borchardt, reported to have been caught in a bottleneck by 250,000 more-heavily-armed Japanese, and to have effected a withdrawal to their west in the direction of Hankow. My expectation was that the Japanese, having gotten the defenders out of Soochow, might not follow them west, choosing first to consolidate their own position on the north-south rail system that connected their older, firmer position in Tientsin in the north with their pivotal, newer position in Nanking in the lower Yangtze valley. I thought they might then approach Hankow by way of the Yangtze. I was right on that one.

Summing Up the First Year

When classes were over in mid-June amidst inconclusive talk about possibly shifting the school to Yuanling for the fall opening, I had a chance to rest up. And I took time to catch up on my journal.

Dylan Thomas would have us "look back, back . . . look back at the black colossal year." I could say that for me the year 1937–38 in Changsha had been stretching and thrilling, all in all a fantastic year, although at its end I was emotionally so drained that my dominant impression was that it had not gone well. I sternly told my diary that I hadn't learned enough Chinese, read enough Chinese history, or investi-

Mr. Shao, school proctor

My most morose class. It took me a long time to erode their hostility.

gated any one thing at sufficient depth. All true, but a fantastic year nonetheless. I had learned my job swiftly, and evolved a workable classroom technique of presenting the lessons clearly with a balance of oral exposition, questioning, reading, and composition. This method had reached its best expression with the III-1, my most friendly and responsive class; and its most troubled expression with II-2, who taught me more than I taught them. My other classes had gone well.

With regard to my photography, although with the country at war I had been understandably timid in pursuing it outside the school, I had made a good photographic record of the school itself. My shortcomings in Chinese history were indeed frustrating, but basically the result of nonavailability of books; however, my compensatory reading of Western classics, such as, Joyce, T. S. Eliot, and Dostoyevski, had been stimulating and meaningful.

I had enjoyed warm contacts with a number of members of the Chinese faculty; and liked my American colleagues very much, the exception being John, my somewhat moody peer, whom I often avoided and whom I only enjoyed when we had a mediating third person with us. There were many interesting acquaintances and new friends, Dr. Liebenthal being the one I took greatest delight in, a man cultivated, gentle, vulnerable and yet poised in his inner wholeness.

I had been much disturbed during the year by being witness to some of the worst aspects of the foreign presence in China — primarily the Japanese aggressors, but also the exploitative role of Western business, foreign gunboats on the river, Western airs of superiority, and the like. I was struck by the primitiveness of Central China in many material ways, but impressed by the polite toughness of its people, friendly and clever, practical and indestructible.

I had taken in a host of visual impressions: the junks with their south-pointing compasses; Mount Nanyo, its pilgrims and beggars; the linguistic complexities of dialect, tone, and brushstroke; the genial unkemptness of temples; the complex admixture of West and East — cars and wheelbarrrows, suits and long gowns, athletics and bound feet; the terror, thrill, and horror of bombings; the variety of troops, good and bad, well and poorly equipped; the beauty of Kwangtung and Hong Kong women; the buttonbright eyes of small children; the placidity of the rice countryside — terraced, manicured, maintained; Hunan's red soil, green fields and blue skies; the absorbing of information about medicine and surgery from Phil Greene, he so eager and so picturesque in his explanations; the witnessing of operations; the ferries, the rickshaws; the endless bartering and haggling; the manufacture of goods in shop fronts; the artificial social eminence of the visiting middle-class American; and the puzzling relationship to coolies and servants. And much more.

Undeniably a year of growth for me.

For the school it was a chopped-up year. The early normalcy had been jarred by air raids and warnings; the fall of Nanking led to the withdrawal of most of our students; January had seen the return of many of them, and from February to June we created a kind of war normalcy. Despite all the vicissitudes, neither student body nor faculty gave up on themselves or the school. Far from being demoralized, and at the same time without grandstanding or heroics, there was a surprising amount of effective teaching and solid studying. Our students ran the Poor School, helped out in the city after raids, and got their work done. The curriculum remained lively and humane; there was none of the legendary barbarism of the English public school — the disproportionate discipline, the floggings and the bullying. The safety record for our school community was fine, with luck for us so far in the location of the air raids.

We did not hear a lot of patriotic hyperbole; and the government, with the exception of two weeks in December, remained blessedly distant. In short, we had been allowed to be ourselves; the school had kept going and was in good shape. Those were not trivial achievements, and, given the distortions of the year, they said a lot not only for the leadership of Principal Lao, Frank Hutchins, and Dean Ying, but for the resilience and determination of all of us, including the departed wives and children of our permanent staff. It took courage to be present; and it took courage to be absent.

Kunming: Summer 1938

The summer vacation offered one of the best opportunities for travel that I would ever have. I wanted a change from Yali and was hoping to cover quite a bit of ground; I was also quite earnestly searching, within whatever novel and interesting experiences I might have, for further insights into China, for the revealing and the representative.

Dr. Liebenthal and I decided to travel together to Kunming in China's southwest where we both could do some tourism and he could try for a position with the refugee northern universities, some of which were attempting to reconstitute themselves there. In that era it was easier and more interesting to get to Kunming by a rather circuitous route. Our departure was by international train for Hong Kong on June 29. We had much difficulty in straightening out our third-class accommodations, ending up in a stray car at the rear, where we joined Charlie Roberts of Changsha's Bible Institute and Borchardt, our military friend then on his way back to Germany. The trip — hot, debilitating, and dirty — created a supreme yearning for ice water and a cool bath. Both of these magically appeared in Kowloon, after the usual chaos of coolies and rickshaw scalpers at the station, when Dr. Liebenthal and I found rooms in the Robinsons' home at 12 Observatory Road. That began a frustrating wait of ten days for ship's passage from Hong Kong to Haiphong, but it also began my exposure to the mysteries of cricket, expounded by Mr. Robinson, and a lifelong friendship with his daughter, Bonnie. The Doktor and

I ultimately secured passage for Haiphong, although departure on the
S.S. Canton meant that we left our ordered haven of ice water, cricket,
and fine cooking for a rusty French vessel of eight hundred tons on a
savage sea. The *Canton* departed in the evening, sailed into the edge of a
typhoon, retreated to Hong Kong harbor until breakfast time, then took
off a second time into seas that may have been less lethal but whose
violence still reduced most of us passengers to wracking nausea for close
to forty-eight hours. With hot meals unthinkable because of my re-
bellious stomach and ice water too risky on a filthy ship because of
dysentery and cholera, the availability of bottled lemonade was a pure,
life-giving miracle. Sunday was insufferable, but I recovered a bit before
regaining terra firma early Tuesday, shaggy of beard and empty of
stomach. I recall being so weak upon arrival in Haiphong that I wondered how I could ever totter through the day, but somehow we dis-
embarked amid baggage and porter turmoil; were passed by customs
without scrutiny; caught the 7 a.m. train for the two-hour trip to Hanoi;
found there a Chinese hotel, noisy, but clean and cheap; and managed to
ingest a late breakfast.

The hotel began a very exotic experience of several days. From our
room on the second floor we looked across a small courtyard upon a
dozen or two young prostitutes who, in the afternoon following siesta,
chattered cheerfully and practiced music loudly on their balcony, the
volume of sound rising in the evening and continuing late into the night.
That constraint on sleep was combined with the need to rise before six to
beat the heat. One slept at midday and surfaced again after siesta for the
relative cool of late afternoon and evening. On those terms life was
tolerable in the heat and humidity of the Red River basin.

The exotic qualities of the hotel were enhanced by our linking up with
someone I will call Gerald, a young English Buddhist who was on his
way to Kunming and who had also come on the *S.S. Canton* from Hong
Kong. Gerald identified himself as a dropout from Cambridge University
and as a member of a prominent English family. He had lived several
years in South China and several more in Peiping, attaining fluency in
both Cantonese and Mandarin, and becoming a Buddhist convert. That
was interesting enough, but I was astonished to learn that this tall,
handsome and self-assured man had an opium habit, and then fascinated

to be invited to watch him smoke. He was articulate, loved to talk, and relished having an interested audience as he lay on his side and prepared his opium for smoking. That ritual consisted of dipping a blunt needle into a viscous fluid like molasses; the tip of the needle with its adhering drop was held briefly over the concentrated heat of a squat opium lamp. He turned the drop as it bubbled and then shaped it on the flat surface near the bowl of the pipe, before dipping the needle tip wth its cooled droplet into the "molasses" once again, the cycle being repeated slowly and peacefully six or eight times. The finished pellet was finally pushed off the needle into the tiny bowl of the opium pipe which was turned to the heat of the lamp so the smoker could ignite the pellet with several big puffs followed by a gigantic long inhale. The whole procedure was known as a "mouth." Since this took place thirty years before the prevalence of drugs in middle-class America, it seemed incredibly exotic and offbeat to me.

Dr. Liebenthal and I visited Gerald a number of times in opium dens to watch and listen. He talked of northern and southern differences in preparation, of the gentleness of the habit, of how he had smoked socially off and on for a year, and even regularly for a month in order to cope with an intestinal ailment, before he realized he had a habit. By the time I knew him he was compelled to smoke two or three "mouths" both morning and evening. He was eager to show us how benign and peaceful the dens were, how civilized smoking was, how unrelated the whole process was to the ill-informed and prejudiced ways in which it was usually perceived by Westerners.

Gerald possessed a romantic image of a perfect and purified Chinese culture that led him to an obsessive conviction that the Chinese way of doing anything—in art, in language, in manners, in dress, in architecture, in agriculture and organization, in religion—was demonstrably the best. Initially, I found this view of life sympathetic, but it risked slipping from novelty and stimulation to tedium and aggravation.

Since both he and Dr. Liebenthal had Buddhist connections, we were, on our second day, up at 5:30 for fried noodles and a lovely rickshaw ride in cool morning air to meet at 7 a.m. two Annamite scholars who took us to visit a temple and a small monastery in the midst of an enormous stand of lotus—a very powerful Buddhist symbol of beauty

123

emergent from mud. We went on to a large and active monastery at the other side of the city where we attended a noisy ceremony, saw part of the monastery, and drank tea with the austere and dignified abbot. It was a quiet setting with graceful trees, a small and slender pagoda, green rice paddies, and a water buffalo at work—all as Chinese as could be, although in Vietnam. We went on to the museum, where I encountered a startlingly different large Kwan Yin (Goddess/God of Mercy, which one sees represented in serene statues over and over in Buddhist temples in China), but this one a nightmare of Hindu-style multiples—many heads against a mandala of scores of arms, like spokes in a carriage wheel. Gerald was a convert to the Tibetan Yellow Sect, as I recall, and felt constrained to defend the sexuality of some of the statues, telling us that Lamaism was less sexual than the statues implied, their grotesque couplings being merely metaphors for the complementary opposites of Yin-Yang. The ardor of the convert led him to genuflect elaborately and to chant prayers in front of each Buddhist statue in the museum before permitting himself to view it with museum eyes. Dr. Liebenthal and I found his exhibitionism embarrassing, but Gerald proceeded, unruffled.

Hanoi itself came through to me as very large, with generally ugly urban architecture low in skyline, with wide well-paved roads and beautiful trees. The cafés offered all the alcoholic advantages of a French city, presumably catering to a large, well-to-do clientele of colonials who must have found a life of luxury there astonishingly cheap by European standards. Soldiers were numerous, and there was plenty of evidence of capital investment. Gerald reported that the city was wide open as far as opium went, and when we went out in the evening, we were badgered by pimps with a broad spectrum of offerings.

One of my touristic first impressions was the omnipresent black teeth, a glossy black in some cases, in a very good-looking population. It came from chewing betel nut—that mixture of folded green leaf, a palm nut, and lime. Another vivid impression was the xylophone sound of loose wooden sandals striking cobblestones, the varied sizes of sandals seemingly tuned differently, their medley a beautiful indication that the city was stirring after siesta. Language sounds were themselves a blend—of Tonkinese, French, and Cantonese, each of them widely used; Annamese, with its quacking and whimpering sounds, was unpleasant to my ears.

Kunming: Summer 1938

Despite the evident presence of an alien French colonial authority, one got the impression of civic order in a viable, functioning city. That was 1938, poignantly close to the war's drastic transformations in Hanoi and the rest of French Indo-China. In 1938 Japan was taking ports in South China, not far to the east of Hanoi; soon, in 1939, France would be caught up in World War II and, in 1940, conquered by Hitler; in that same period Japan would begin her moves onto the Indo-China coast to protect her oil sources in the south; in 1941, Pearl Harbor; in 1942 Japan would move massively into Indo-China, retaining until near the end of the war the same French colonial apparatus that probably filled Indo-Chinese nationalists with despair but that in 1938 conveyed to me a sense of civic order. The nightmare of those years led on into the postwar civil war and the struggle for independence, the ghastly confrontation of Vietnam with the U.S., and the dislocations, problems, and brutalities accompanying Hanoi's victorious leadership.

.   .   .

We left by train for Yünnan province in China on the evening of July 15 after four strenuous days in Hanoi. Our modest hotel handled all our luggage safely and expertly, and we found ourselves on the 8 p.m. train in a small, third-class carriage, confronting a night with no place to rest our heads except the windowsill. Gerald had perfected an inexpensive and modish style of travel in which his luggage awarded precedence to luxuries over necessities, his theory being that basics were obtainable as he went along, relieving him of the need to carry them, whereas selected luxuries, often unobtainable unless he carried them, made possible a civilized enjoyment of travel in the midst of its inevitable discomforts. As the train jostled us along through the night, past banana plantations and jungle, he produced a handsome teapot, several small and elegant cups, which we were expected to admire, and a canister of carefully chosen green tea. Hot water, always available either on the train or in a station, gave him all he needed to serve us repeated cups of first-rate tea. Those night hours yielded to a full day on the train which began with an early crossing of the Chinese border into Yünnan province and took us past more jungle and a million bananas, up and up slowly on one of the most remarkable narrow-gauge ascents in the world, a line which had been built a generation earlier with French capital and at a cost of fearful malaria for the labor force. We had wonderful scenery with silver water falls and grand rolling hills, cultivated high on their flanks; there were hundreds of trestles and tunnels and tortuous twistings past small stations, an endless eating of bananas, and occasional standing on the platform at the end of the car to watch the bending of the long train, still miraculously on its hazardous track. Finally, we emerged onto the plateau and were once again among relatively small and manageable hills, with a view in the late afternoon sun over a flat and fertile plain, dramatically juxtaposed to the valley scenery of our entire day. The plain contained the yellows and greens of flourishing crops, the chocolate-red of newly ploughed earth, scattered gray villages with overhanging trees, and the central city of Meng Tze — small and placid, all contributed to a beauty that brought me a rush of secret joy, one of those sudden, welcome, unpredictable hours of total happiness; this, in the remote town of K'ai Yuen, where the train put us down for the night. We found a simple, clean hotel near the station and just outside the town wall, our room facing the courtyard with a tree in blossom. After supper Gerald and I ventured out in the dark, onto a paved road next to the town wall, where blossoming trees perfumed our walk to the towering town gate. Entering the gate, we walked for a quarter of an hour through streets that were utterly and traditionally Chinese, seemingly as untouched by modern China as by the outside world. Here was Gerald's distilled, purified, innermost China; and for me the delight of listening to his romantic approvals, presented in beautiful English, and an incomparable glimpse into a remote traditionalism, all a fantastic reward in my search for the quintessential Chineseness of China. It was a magic casement for us both. After a slow retracing of our perfumed route, I had an hour of talk with him while he smoked his evening "mouths," and then fell into bed at ten to sleep well and deeply.

The hotel servants woke us at 4:30 a.m. so we could wash, eat breakfast, and get ourselves and our luggage onto the train by its 6:30 departure for Kunming, capital of the province. All day long we lumbered across the plateau, following a brown stream — evidence of recent heavy rains — with high rocky hills on either side and glimpses of distant villages. At one point where a small landslide covered the tracks, we carried our baggage around to another train which had us in Kunming in a couple of hours.

·　　·　　·

Gerald's passionate search to identify inexpensively with the real China led us this time to a merchants' inn whose modest two stories and two open courtyards offered food, shelter, and a panorama of city life for about nine American cents each day. The outer courtyard provided strings of ponies with rest and fodder, and merchants with storage space for their parcels and bales. Our room on the second floor opened onto a balcony overlooking the noisy inner courtyard where on a number of simple tables identical and very good meals were served at 9 a.m. and 4 p.m. Victrola renderings of Peiping opera were on day and night; conversation was often loud, late into the night, with a monkey, tethered to a post, adding his own occasional comments; and vendors of brushes, snacks, and various other articles hawked their wares with traditional street cries. It was so Elizabethan, Shakespeare would have felt at home. Our room, dirty and spartan, contained as a bed just basic planks over sawhorses. Tea was constantly served; the smoking of tobacco was universal; opium, cheap and of good quality, was available in a den under our room.

If Hanoi was an exotic blend of East and West, Kunming seemed solidly Chinese. It was the final destination of the French-built rail line up from Hanoi, and all of Yünnan province lay within the French economic sphere of influence in China, assuring priority to French banks, French railroaders, and French mining interests. But French influence was not only largely invisible but approaching its demise when the whole structure of Europe's "unequal treaties" was soon to be wiped out as a result of the war. Kunming in 1938 still had a pristine, unmodified, true-blue look about it. The Burma road, of which Kunming soon became the terminus, had not been thought of; there was a modest airfield, but the American air base would appear half-a-dozen years hence. Within the city walls, there were few foreigners, no European sector, no Europeanized or Americanized shops, few buildings of foreign design. People walked or rode rickshaws, and goods were carried or moved by pony. A few public buses took people to the airport, but no private cars were to be seen. The cobblestones really belonged to the pedestrians. Among the big Chinese cities which I visited, Kunming was the most consistently Chinese in architecture, structure, and atmosphere, and the least modified by treaty port influences.

This was a city ornamented by Wu San-kwei, grandee of the southwest and military traitor, who, in the mid-seventeenth century, first helped the Manchus to breach the Great Wall and thus enter and conquer China. Wu was then splendidly rewarded with control of a large satrapy in Kunming and the southwest, from which he mounted a major challenge to the authority of the Emperor in distant Peiping. The northern part of the city was most reminiscent of the grandeur that was Kunming in the seventeenth century. The park on a rise of land gave a fine view toward mountains in the middle distance, and — below — a large Buddhist complex of temples, cloisters, and bridges, palatial in layout. The buildings, despite faded paint and inadequate upkeep, suggested Peiping's grandeur, much imitated by Wu San-kwei. Wood, a rarity in a generally treeless country, was used for glory and display in these buildings. The marble bridges, with incised designs on the balustrading, were right out of Peiping palace architecture — which I saw the following summer — as were the use of terraces, cloisters, tile roofs, balcony design, and the painted columns and eaves. Wu San-kwei, by this evidence, seemed not only ambitious but homesick for the North. However, when Peiping ordered him to the capital, this turbulent dissident wisely found reasons not to comply.

Kunming did more to open my eyes to China than any other of my Chinese experiences. The chief reason was the presence of Gerald, who pointed out much to me that otherwise would have escaped my notice. But, sadly, our relationship soured. Dr. Liebenthal, tiring of him sooner than I, was careful to keep his distance by lodging at another hotel. Although Gerald had been immensely stimulating, the two weeks of rooming together was an overexposure for us both. He was bothered by my American bursts of laughter, by my argumentative reluctance to accept and identify with everything Chinese, and perhaps most of all by my slapping of mosquitoes in the bedroom, each of them possibly the bearer of a transmigrant Buddhist soul. In defense of my crass actions, my plea is that the mosquitoes were abundant; that we were not far from a dangerous malaria region; and Gerald had a grand mosquito net while I had none. It was like a Graham Greene scene. I came to find irritating the pontifical insistence on his point of view and his total lack of a sense of humor. The last straw was the discovery that he had picked up gonorrhea. He had said that his Buddhist vows forbade sexual relations

Top: Kunming: another glimpse into quintessential China: City gate (left), unobtrusive policeman (left), cobblestones, pedestrians, rickshaws, upturned eaves, ornamental windows.

Kunming: grand ornamental wooden "arches," each with tile roof and built-up eaves, on a beautiful main thoroughfare that in 1938 was still unviolated by the automobile. Kunming was the provincial capital and the most prominent city of the entire southwest.

Top: Kunming: poverty row just outside a section of the city wall, and backed against it; the wall just discernible through the confusion of grass on top of it. The wall's dilapidation is evident in the grass and shrubs on the roof.

Left: Kunming: Peiping-style city gate—grand, handsome, dignified.

Peasant, plough power and abudant water, all essentials in the cultivation of rice, are here juxtaposed to the rice itself in the upper right. My search for the heart of China had no greater reward than this sight of a wary but unintimidated boy with an unconcerned water buffalo. This immemorial and indispensable animal, during ploughing season up to his belly in mud and water, was used to prepare the rice paddies for planting. I was told repeatedly how much water buffaloes hated foreigners and would attack without provocation. The presumption was that meat-eating foreigners—as opposed to basically vegetarian Asiatics—had aggressive body odors that buffaloes found intolerable. This one tolerated mine.

For me one of the special places in Kunming was this old pagoda with a crown of foliage in which dark-eared kites nested. The pagoda is mentioned in Marco Polo's account of his visit to this city in the late thirteenth century.

with women, but not with small boys, although his opium habit, he added, so reduced his sexual desire as to eliminate the latter. He insisted over and over again to the physician to whom he went and to me, that the only way he could have picked up the disease was from a random, innocent contact. So obsessed was he with that point that I had no peace until I yielded to his hammering insistence and said I believed him. I knew very little about the disease, but was filled with uneasiness over living next to someone who insisted he had come by it through innocent proximity, precisely the circumstance of our own living arrangements. Dr. Liebenthal, again sooner than I, concluded that Gerald was a liar in this and other matters, as the Chinese commonly believed opium addicts to be. Whatever the case, our relations, after two weeks in that hotel room, had so many complex shadings of like and dislike, of stimulation and stress, as to be bewildering to me. It was a tremendous relief to leave early in August.

I decided to fly to Chungking and try to secure passage by riverboat into western Szechuan province, so I could go on a pilgrimage to Mount Omei, one of China's sacred Buddhist mountains.

Trip by Junk

On innumerable occasions during my two years in China I ran into local scenes and situations that cried out for lingering, loving, detailed scrutiny by the camera's eye. Most were situations where I couldn't linger or where I needed an interpreter to cope with the local dialect, or where I needed to be more brazen in my approach. I could take a step in the direction of such photographic essays on this trip where I had the boat as a photographer's blind.

Dr. Liebenthal and I went on a very satisfying local trip to West Mountain, which is seen from Kunming, the lake visible at the foot of the mountain. The Doktor called for me at 8 a.m., and we walked to the little West Gate area with its lively wholesale market and pigs, ponies, handlers, boat people, and much haggling over sales.

The busy Kunming waterfront.

There were tribal women standing about, identifiable by different hairdos and in some cases by tribal dress. This was a sight denied us in Changsha, but to be had in towns of Kweichow and Yunnan provinces in Southwest China. When one considers the tremendous absorptive powers of Chinese civilization, reinforced by its population pressures, it is surprising how many areas of separate tribal cultural identity remain in China. There are reported to be over eighty such groups in Kweichow alone. We foreigners, like the Chinese themselves, tended to move exclusively within the Chinese orbit: contacts with the Lolo and Miao were possible but required special rural trips and arrangements that one was unlikely to make.

The canal took us past a curious set of rural buildings, more substantial in tile roof and masonry walls than rural dwellings in the Hunanese countryside near Changsha. Also unlike Hunan, there were a number of circular storage structures under thatch, behind the women pounding and rinsing the family wash.

Above: We bargained with a boat family and engaged them and their craft for the day. The view here is from the inside of the junk before our departure. Take away the ubiquitous felt hat, supply the men with queues, and this scene could have occurred two or three centuries earlier. The central figure holds a bamboo water pipe of the type often seen in Southwest China.

Opposite top: Our ancient transport in this basic South China setting was run by a smiling, hard-working family. The craft was simple, tough, durable; the family lived on the boat and was reasonably snug in wet weather under the arched panels of bamboo matting; oars were handled efficiently in standing position with forward body-thrust, the baby piggyback and quiet on the mother's back most of the day. The mast was un-stepped for ease in going down the canal and stowed at right, a wok just below it.

Opposite bottom: The father took the bow oar as we headed down the canal. This was the view which Dr. Liebenthal and I had as we sat low in the shade of the arched covers. The passage, one way, to West Mountain took about two hours.

Above: When there was a possibility of the junk's cover scraping as we passed under the loose plank of a small footbridge, a shout brought from the dwelling on the left, with its ramshackle combination of thatch and tile roof, an adult who lifted the plank enough for clearance. Her facial covering made us wonder if she were a leper.

Opposite page: This, I feel, was one of my most startling shots. We encountered and passed this couple who were operating a sampan that had come in off the lake and was headed down the canal to Kunming with a cargo of cobblestones or bricks, so overloaded that it had about one inch of freeboard between gunwale and water. The load had been carefully balanced, nevertheless waves no more than an inch and a quarter high threatened constantly to fill their craft and drop it to the bottom in a matter of seconds. Boat people were said not to know how to swim.

The Chinese, their ingenuity inexhaustible, had made the transportation of heavy and awkward loads one of their fine arts. I watched one man carry three thick bamboo poles, each twenty-five feet or more in length, fully four inches thick at one end, and potentially very awkward. The solution was extremely simple. Tied closely together at their small ends and several feet apart at their large ends the poles formed a loose tripod on its side: one pole rested at its point of balance on his shoulder, the other two poles were steadied by his hands at waist level. All three were off the ground and under control.

Or take the commonest sight of all, the shoulder carrying stick with a water bucket suspended from each end. The novice, thinking this the simplest of carrying acts — as in a way it is — can send himself sprawling if he doesn't move with rhythmic exactness in a step slower than normal walking or in an alternative quick step, each ordained by the flexing of the carrying stick. It is undoubtedly the most efficient way in the world to carry that amount of weight, a method that to the Chinese makes the relative inefficiency of suitcases laughable.

Another small family junk. This one moved by mother and children with mast stepped and narrow sail up as a help in crossing the lake. Here on the plateau the climate was livable and temperate, the clouds in the rainy season were dramatic, and the interplay of city, canal, villages, lakes, hills, and mountains was inexhaustibly beautiful and satisfying.

We left our boat family for several hours as we climbed halfway up the mountain. From there we followed a good path to visit a Buddhist temple, where we had soup and noodles and a rest before walking on to the steep tumble of Taoist temples near the cliff. These are two Buddhist temple guardians.

From the cliff itself we had this stirring view back over the lake toward the city, showing the exquisite juxtaposing of lake, land, and cumulus clouds. We took a steep descent trail down to the water and walked along the shore back to our waiting boat.
Tired, we were ready for the two hours of quiet locomotion homeward to Kunming.
All in all, this was one of the best day-trips of a lifetime, although it ended with typical China irony in supper at the little West Gate where the flies were so omnipresent
and maddeningly persistent that, if we weren't careful, they would land on our
chopsticks between plate and mouth.

Omei, Pilgrimage Mountain

I lay awake most of the last night in Kunming in fear of over-sleeping, finally leaving the little inn by 5:30 a.m., joined by Dr. Lie-benthal, who came to see me off. We ate nearby and drove in a large bus out the south end of the city, past the Sanskrit Temple where, on one of our walks, he had displayed his impressive language skills a few days earlier. We soon covered the several miles to the airport, which was already alive with the sounds of planes.

I took a port seat aft on the plane to Chungking where my vision would be unobstructed by the wings, waved good-bye to the Doktor, and was shortly above the Kunming Plateau with surpassingly beautiful views of the courtyard architectural patterns of the city, the rich cultivation and the village clusters, West Mountain and the lake. I watched the dazzling choreography of well-defined cloud formations, at one point our plane flying between layers not more than one hundred fifty feet apart. At length the landscape became visible again, rough, hilly country with isolated dwellings on small, purplish-red hills surrounded by green and yellow fields and by rice paddies of every shape in the valleys. The pattern was quite different from that of the villages around Kunming. I saw a curious system of domed sandstone ridges facing each other, meeting in an ellipse covered with a quilt of rice paddies, all high above the surrounding valley. We soon picked up the Yangtze and followed it east to the island airport upstream from Chungking. It was the first flight of a new route, a three-hour trip from the coolness of Yünnan to the sweltering midsummer heat of Szechuan, from my priceless Doktor to the possibility of never seeing him again, from the interest of Kunming to the architectural ugliness of wartime Chungking. I wondered whatever could have possessed me when I chose to make such a shift. After casting about, I luckily found refuge at Gordon Jones' Canadian Mission Agency — the Agency — with an excellent view of the waterfront from my bed on the porch and the city's best exposure to what few breezes there were.

.   .   .

In the dark of Wednesday night I made a Hollywood-style, clandestine departure by chair along the battlements of the river wall, winding and turning, up and down endless steps, to the Ming Sen wharf. As romantic a trip as I ever hope to take, but blighted by an upset stomach. When, after a night on the boat at dock, my stomach still ached, I retreated to the Canadian Mission with the aid of Mr. Meng of West China University. God bless him!

The riverboats seemed so complicated that I gave up the idea of a grand trip to western Szechuan, made a plane reservation for Hunan for a week hence, and settled down to read a beautiful folio edition of *The Seven Pillars of Wisdom*. However, since I was feeling well on Saturday when Dr. Stuart Allen, a Canadian missionary surgeon en route to Mt. Omei, uncovered a possible boat passage, I cancelled the plane and joined him, planting my newly purchased camp bed on board the *Ming Fu* Saturday morning and sleeping on it that night in preparation for the Sunday departure.

We were comfortably cool on the lower deck in the cheapest location ($20 Mex) on the ship, but were confined to our beds because of the severe crowding, and bothered by flies. The food was edible, the landscape pleasant, and the boat rather fast, considering the formidable current. I was dismayed to have forgotten my copies of Sophocles and Dostoevski's *The Possessed*, which I had purposely brought from Kunming for this trip. That lengthened each day's unwelcome, enforced lying-down, but by our oversleeping we won the precious freedom of walking at mooring time each evening. Sitting in tea shops was inhibited

146

Part of my waterfront view in Chungking. The breeze was welcomed by me in the August heat, as well as by these large river craft headed upstream against the muscle of the Yangtze.

on our first evening when we were warned not to leave the village beach because a gang of army deserters was known to be in the vicinity. We walked up and down near the *Ming Fu*, as paper cash offerings to the spirits of ancestors and departed relatives were being burned by worshippers near us on the shore.

We ate ashore and spent part of the late afternoon and several hours again in the evening sitting and talking in tea shops. For two cents one could sit there endlessly, eat watermelon seeds, drink tea, arrange business deals, or simply talk. Every adult in town seemed to drop in. With many and various tea shops, friends had some choice as to where to gather. The whole scene with its laughter and animation called to mind what I had read about the conversation and bustle of London's eighteenth-century coffee houses.

Back on the ship, someone announced before our arrival at Suifu that we must change boats there for Kiating. Told that the boat would be half the size of the *Ming Fu*, we readied ourselves to struggle for space on it.

Upper Yangtze

After such preparation and some hours of waiting, we discovered that our boat would after all take us through to Kiating—a great blessing.

While tied up in Suifu we called on Dr. and Mrs. Charles Tompkins, who had spent thirty-five years there at the Baptist Hospital. We were invited by them to share a Western supper in their garden under a waxing moon. Cut off from the world, the Tompkinses were avid for any and all news we could produce. Their returns from furlough had normally required two months of travel on the Yangtze alone, but in the preceding January they had come in from Hong Kong by plane in a matter of hours, almost forgetting their fear of the swift and brutal Yangtze which appeared only an innocent, winding ribbon below their plane window.

We returned to the *Ming Fu* for a sleepless night, the result—we thought — of food eaten earlier on the ship. From my perch in the primitive toilet I could see moonlight over the junction just below us where the Min and Yangtze met.

.   .   .

Scenery on the Min River was more beautiful and the river narrower — a mere one hundred yards in some places — but life on the ship went on much as before. While we exhausted ourselves by constant lying down, the *Ming Fu* passed junks which were being laboriously hauled upriver by trackers — groups of men on the riverbank with long bamboo ropes. We occasionally saw a village or a pagoda or a sandstone cliff; babies cried, meals appeared, and the *Ming Fu* now and then churned slowly to enable a sampan passenger to climb aboard. The countryside itself had many small rolling hills, some with that rarity in the China of that era — trees — others with bamboo clumps, and still others wet-terraced for rice or dry-terraced for kaoliang, something like American corn.

My route from Chungking up the Yangtze and then north up the Min describes an arc which borders and defines the southern edge of the Red Basin. The basin itself is an agricultural and botanical paradise, combining good soil, abundant water, skilled irrigation, a great range of climate zones, and a phenomenal variety of crops and plants.

Approaching Kiating about noon, someone called out that the two-hundred-foot stone Buddha was visible, causing a stampede of passengers to the shore rail with a frightening list to starboard. Dr. Allen quickly and efficiently got us off and ashore via a sampan, leaving the baggage for his servants; we learned that two men were drowned soon after we left when one of the sampans overturned.

We had some good, hot Szechuanese food, and spent the afternoon in and about Dr. Allen's old home and hospital. He took me to some of the Mantse Caves, believed to have been inhabited by ancient man. In the evening I bought embroidery, clothes, and carvings before getting to bed early, in preparation for an early start.

Up at 5:00 for a 6:00 o'clock departure, getting from the hospital hill a splendid view of the cliffs of Mt. Omei, we hired *hwagrs* as we went along. The *hwagr* was a local, mountain conveyance unknown to me; it consisted of two long bamboo poles placed on the shoulders of fore and

Dr. Allen, Canadian medical missionary in Szechuan — my companion on the upper Yangtze, on the Min, and overland to Mt. Omei.

aft porters. Suspended from the middle, and susceptible to the rhythm of bending bamboo, was the simplest of canvas seats and a swinging bamboo footrest suspended by two strings. For comfort and efficiency of design the *hwagr* is without equal the world over. We stopped for breakfast and a rest for the porters, and were at the foot of Omei for luncheon.

Dr. Allen branched off towards Hsin Kai Sse, where his wife and children had a cottage for part of the summer in the small foreign enclave. I started on foot an hour later, with a sturdy boy carrying my baggage, which by now included a sack of peanuts and a large live chicken, both recommended by the doctor as food supplements for the monastic diet ahead of me. We made it by suppertime to Tao Wo Sse, part way up the mountain, and stopped for the night at the monastery, my chicken being released to forage for itself. Supper led to a stomachache, diarrhea, and a sleepless night, but I was well enough by morning to continue, except that my boy had abandoned me. It took me a while to find another and to hire a mountain *hwagr* by which time my chicken had developed a talent for eluding me. Unsuccessful in several attempts to catch it and embarrassed by publicizing further in this citadel of

Yangtze, on the Min, and overland to Mt. Omei.

Typical town waterfront, upriver from Chungking.

devout pilgrimage my un-Buddhist designs on it, I left the chicken and
went on up the mountain.

.   .   .

We followed the valley up, began steep climbing on steps and paused for
lunch at one of the scores of temples. As we went on I walked the steep
sections and rode the *hwagr* on the easy parts. Our path took us through
a series of small gorges, the men sometimes wading up to their knees in
swift water. We stopped for grand views up and down, many over dense
forest cover — fantastically precious and moving vistas in generally treeless China. We made Gio Lao Tung (Cave of the Nine Sages) by 4 p.m.
for overnight.

With ample time before supper, I got into clean clothes and strolled to
the tunnel-like caves, going down into the mountain along damp confin-
ing corridors accompanied by a surly monk with only a saucer of oil, a
wick, and a tiny flickering flame to hold the darkness at bay. Thousands
of large alpine swifts poured past us in the blackness, often only inches
from our faces. Among the fastest birds in the world, their hurtling speed
so close to my eyes was unsettling. We trudged to an unprepossessing
shrine seemingly well inside this upper part of the mountain, a spot held
by tradition to have had religious connections with ancient-ancient
society in China. I found its special remoteness so unnerving that it gave
me palpitations. Walking back, I found that half-light at the end of the
tunnel was never so welcome, although the large, high-speed swifts, now
dimly visible, were just as intimidating as they had been in the dark.

At the monastery I was drafted by the host monk to paint English
words on a sign pointing to the cave. Bringing the special guestbook for
me to sign, he was all attentiveness and charm, putting on pressure for a
generous contribution to the monastery — and blissfully unaware of my
near-prostrate financial posture. When, at departure the following morning, I left the acceptable minimum, all that I could afford, he snatched it
from my hand and turned his back on me, a picture of rudeness and
disappointment. It was one of those scenes whose embarrassment is
impossible to forget. He was bitter; and I chagrined not to have planned
my money better.

Stone Buddha, said to be two hundred feet tall, carved in the living rock, across from Kiating on the Min River.

Up at six for a seven o'clock start, our route offering a great view at first, but from a harrowing path along the face of a cliff. Then the mist closed in on us. Later we — the porters and I — encountered and climbed stone steps, thousands of them, before stopping for lunch at a temple where the vista was still denied by cloud and light rain, but where we were warmed by a charcoal fire. We soon set off again by paths and steps; I mostly by *hwagr*.

The monastery buildings at or near the summit I found astonishing. Their heavily-weathered wooden exteriors resembled unpainted Vermont barns, but the roofs often had deep, old rich thatch in which plants, and even shrubs, grew. Their entangling root systems must have helped keep the lid on in storms; all the same, shrubs overhead on top of Mt. Omei were surprising. All these externals existed in astonishing juxtaposition to the ornate interiors of the worship areas.

These remarkable structures and communities were among scores of shrines, temples, and monasteries clustered on this most Buddhist of mountains in China's most Buddhist of provinces. Many of those structures celebrated in painting and sculpture the achievements of Pu Hsien, the pioneer Indian Buddhist who in the seventh century came on elephant through the chaos of mountains to the west of where I stood and, upon arriving here, made Mt. Omei his base and study center. Buddhism, unlike nineteenth century Christianity, typically spread through such worship and study centers, without evangelization. Pu Hsien, if indeed it is correct that he played the key pioneer role as bearer of the Buddhist message to Szechuan, was by his impact the most effective unevangelical missionary in history.

At the Gin Din, the summit monastery, mist, light rain and a simple, comfortable room awaited me. With monastery routines of worship, training, meditation, and work flowing on around me, I settled in, walked about with my head in the clouds, had supper, and went to bed.

I got up in the middle of the night to see the moon but mist enveloped everything. At six I walked to the top in a light rain and still saw only mist. At seven I went back, climbed those final steps and turned around expecting once again to see nothing. This time I was rewarded — there, on the far side of a cottony sea of low clouds, emerged the white shoulders and peaks of the Snow Mountains, backed by a light blue sky and topped by a high cloud ceiling. The ragged summit of Minya Gonka appeared about the same height as Omei, but at twenty-five thousand feet it was more than twice as high. In the clear air of that moment it seemed startlingly close, although some ninety miles to the west in Sikang province. A great sight, worth all the drawn-out planning and effort.

If God presented himself anywhere to me it was in the beauty, the quiet, and the grandeur of nature. I had often wondered why religionists of different faiths couldn't more readily and happily fit together in their spiritual joys. Here, I could easily identify with the Buddhist pilgrim.

I remained three days at the top, visiting the nearby temples and monasteries. I tried repeatedly to see the Buddha's Glory, over the precipice on the north side of the summit. There, between 2 and 3 p.m., if the clouds are close below when the sun is at an appropriate height in the south, the pious pilgrim standing at the edge of the precipice can thrill to the sight of this light phenomenon.

Buddha's Glory had not been visible for a month, but just before my departure I was privileged to witness it. There below me on the clouds was the dark profile of the Buddha surrounded by a bright halo. The thrill of this sight is believed to have moved many devotees over the centuries to throw themselves over the precipice into the loving arms of the Buddha. It was indeed thrilling to see this celebrated halo, although I prosaically resisted the impulse to jump.

What the pilgrim really sees is the shadow of his own head and shoulders on the cloud below him with a lovely concentration of light around his head, that halo being visible only to himself. In *Tess of the D'Urbervilles* Thomas Hardy described a scene in which, as several persons walked down a field-path, "there moved onward with them, around the shadow of each one's head a circle of opalized light, formed by the moon's rays upon the glistening sheet of dew. Each pedestrian could see no halo but his or her own, which never deserted the head-shadow, . . . but . . . persistently beautified it." Anyone walking soon after sunrise through grass heavy with dew, can observe a small, sparkling halo around the shadow of his head, a perpetually pleasant link with Mt. Omei and a comforting reminder that Buddha's Glory is around us and goes with us.

Above: Mount Omei had in 1938 scores of active Buddhist establishments — temples, shrines, and monasteries. About ten thousand feet high, Omei was on the eastern fringe of a densely mountainous region difficult of access, much of it wilderness.

Left: The temples and monasteries near the summit were barnlike, with unpainted, weathered, wooden exteriors; some had old thatch with growing grass and shrubs in it, probably helpful in severe weather.

Looking up toward the summit of Mount Omei. From the monastery complex at the summit the view is west toward Minyar Gonka, the snow mountains. It was through this mountain wilderness that Pu Hsien and his elephant are believed to have come to Omei.

Law and order at the foot of Mount Omei: the pole and its raised carrier were the traditional means of displaying the heads of criminals, although none was evident here.

. . .

I left the summit right after my view of Buddha's Glory. There was rain on the way down, but wonderful monasteries to visit. I was overnight at Si Hsiang Sse, and later saw for the first time a troop of wild monkeys. Stopping at Da Wo Sse again, I encountered my abandoned chicken. I chased and collected the chicken and added it to my luggage for the walk of several miles to the Allens' summer home at Hsin Kai Sse.

During this interlude at the Allens', innumerable cicadas maintained a ceaseless, rasping, incredible, gear-grinding, ear-splitting torment, the like of which I had never heard.

Miss Eleanor Graham of the Women's Missionary Society (United Church of Canada), Marie Hoffman, wife of Dr. Cecil Hoffman, the superintendent of the Canadian Hospital in Chungking, her two young children, Dorothea and Beverly accompanied by their amah, and I set out together by *hwagrs* to Omei Hsien, then to a river town where we took a junk down to Kiating for overnight. Next day we all squeezed on the small, crowded steamer for Chungking.

Marie Hoffman, Canadian missionary; with one of her children and the child's amah. Boatman in the rear inching his craft upstream against the relentless Yangtze.

This time I slept on the upper deck where I luxuriated for three days in the smiling weather and the fascination of those stone-stepped water-fronts and the abundant river traffic. The big river craft with their massive sweeps, workaday design, and general clumsiness required nice handling in the tangled crosscurrents of the Min and upper Yangtze. Moving a medium-sized or small craft against the current along any of those waterfronts involved clawing one's way along by boathook, a foot at a time.

The innumerable stone steps at the Chungking waterfront were dramatic evidence of that city's relationship to the river—the radical changes, often within the day, in the height of the water, commonly involving twenty or thirty feet, sometimes sixty or seventy, comparable to the highest tides in the world. When we arrived the river was at twenty-seven feet, very low; two weeks earlier it had been eighty feet; at some point in the summer it often goes up to one hundred feet. These startling changes were the product of a large catchment area which had rain but virtually no forest cover to slow down the runoff. As the upper

On the upper Yangtze—one always had to deal with the overwhelming fact of the remorseless current.

Yangtze was confined by hills to an inelastic width, the runoff resulted in quick ups and downs.

To deal efficiently with these variations the waterfront has to have facilities of constantly adjustable height and nonrotting durability. The answer has been thousands of stone steps that offer workable mooring and good footing for passengers stepping off the sampan ferries. The stone can survive the constant wetness either from inundation by the river or from the dripping water buckets carried by thousands of water coolies from the river up to neighborhood cisterns for the city's water supply.

The Gorges

Just a few days in Chungking at the Agency so I could change money, eat some ice cream, and see Rocky Chin, who was then employed in Chungking by the Kuo Li Bien I Kuan (National Institute for Compilation and Translation). He was making a gallant attempt to accommodate his highly Americanized identity with the mainstream activities of wartorn China. Despite willingness and sensitivity, he would inevitably remain an outsider.

Tens of thousands of refugees from the eastern half of China — university personnel, government officials, businessmen and bankers, prostitutes and beggars — were crowding into Chungking. This unloved and unlovely city was crammed into a peninsula of hilly land between two rivers, the Yangtze on its southeast and the Chia-ling on its northwest. These were cruel constraints for a city soon to have dozens of savage air raids. Although the raids had not yet begun, no one doubted their imminence. These bridgeless rivers made it impossible for pedestrians to get out of the city except by a limited number of streets that went southwest and on which crowds of pedestrians had to compete with sedan chairs, rickshaws, and some automobiles.

Escape from the city was also possible by crossing the Yangtze via sampan-ferry or hired sampan to the relative safety of the countrified southeast shore. Large numbers could not be evacuated quickly in that fashion, nor could sampan owners be prevented from bargaining for scalpers' prices in times of emergency.

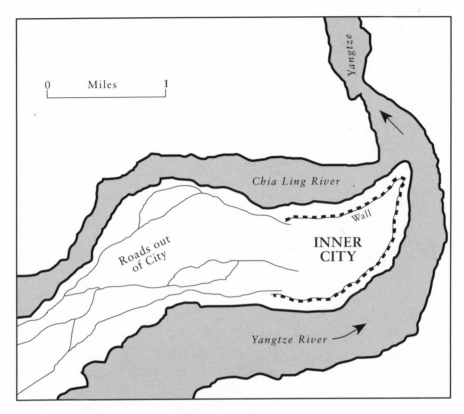

Chungking

A seemingly innocent fact was the inevitable presence of gray roof tiles on every building in Chungking. They lay, overlapped and unfastened, in parallel, sloping, adjacent rows, with every two concave courses linked and made watertight by a convex course. An admirable, traditional system, entirely consonant with the Chinese reverence for simplicity — and utterly unsuited to the disasters of modern war, where one bomb could bring down a neighborhood full of heavy, entrapping tiles, this in a city where egress was already compromised by the rivers.

· · ·

Off from Chungking, downstream this time, passing yet another unusual Buddhist site — Shih Pao Chai, with its tiered, pagoda-like stories fastened to the cliff face of a monadnock shaped like a loaf of bread — we were headed toward the most celebrated river scenery in China, the

The Gorges

Yangtze Gorges, a mountainous area through which the river poured its might, sometimes at twelve to fourteen knots, toward the flatter regions of southern Hupeh, northern Hunan, and points east. The steamers that worked the gorges had been specially designed by a British engineer about a generation earlier. With big engines and small passengers' quarters they served as a river express between Hankow and Chungking.

When we tied up for the night at the river town of Wanhsien and I emerged from the daytime confinement of my folding cot to stretch my legs in town and park, I ran into a young Ginling faculty group with Ettie Chin, Rocky's sister, among them. Ettie had gone to Smith and Michigan and was teaching physical education at Ginling.

They were part of the westward, wartime flight of China's colleges and universities, most of which had grown up in the more cosmopolitan and more sophisticated eastern half of China, and many of which were now shifting into cramped temporary quarters in the west. These girls, hoping to escape the miseries of Japanese occupation, were headed into a swarm of physical, financial, and spiritual problems as their college relocated in Chengtu, where they expected to share the pre-existing campus of West China Union University with some other colleges. I later heard that many students couldn't stand the strain of inadequate food, air-raid interruptions, increased incidence of TB, and inflation, and that there were numerous student deaths, often by suicide.

For our downstream transit of the gorges we stood out in the middle of the river, let our engine roar to maintain headway in the tricky, racing waters of those narrows, and then moved so swiftly that I found it difficult not only to decide what to photograph, but to keep track of changes of light from the clouds and snap my composition before I lost it. There was also the standard photographer's dilemma: the difficulty of taking in the scenery while concentrating on photographing it.

An upstream trip would have been physically and spiritually different. For one thing it might have required three weeks instead of three days. The small steamer would have hugged the shore to avoid the greater current of midstream. Even there the current might have been so powerful in some sections that the boat's thundering engine would have barely maintained steerage. If it lost headway, as sometimes happened, the craft would be out of control on a temperamental river that had devoured dozens of steamers, to say nothing of thousands of junks. Upstream progress for both steamer or junk was sometimes measured in millimeters and made possible only with scores of trackers from the nearby river villages. One could see their paths on the steep banks at several different levels, enabling them to deal with different heights of water. The fat hawser from ship to shore, traditionally woven of bamboo, was still in use in my era. To it were attached the individual trackers' smaller ropes that could be tapped by the foreman's baton to test for honest effort. If the tracker's rope was taut, he was clearly pulling hard. The endless time of the upstream struggle sometimes granted the passengers prolonged views of the monkeys that lived like goats on the cliff faces. The gorge water was so abnormally low in the summer of 1937 that my Changsha friend George Helde of the YMCA, going west, took the plane rather than risk the riverboat tangling with one of the myriad wrecks that lurked under the surface of the Yangtze.

John Hersey in *A Single Pebble* (Knopf, 1956) has given us the gripping details of the traditional upstream transit by one of the big, commercial river junks. For his river people the upstream ordeal ended at the town of Wanhsien. For me, on the downriver run, Wanhsien began the experience of the gorges. Below the town we entered the celebrated Wind Box Gorge, and, later, passed through the beautiful Witch's Mountain Gorge. Each was attended by stretches of treacherous rapids that altered and shifted according to the Yangtze's height of water. High water normally came in the spring, its speed and volume greatly increasing the problems of the trackers. We thundered on down the racing water and without mishap traversed the last gorge: Yellow Cat. Thereafter, peace and quiet accompanied us to port.

That exposure to time and the river gave me a lasting appreciation not only of the power of the river but also of the profundity of the movement from East to West China. The river itself posed so many problems that it was at best a meager avenue westward through the barricading mountains of Central China. To the east of the mountain barrier was Ichang, the last river city in Central China that was easy of access, a transshipment waterfront for westbound people and goods about to enter the gorges; to the west of the mountains was Chungking, a crossroads point for almost everyone and everything in the Red Basin of Szechuan. It was a momentous development for both halves of China to have so many highly talented Easterners moving for safety into China's west. With them went the proximity of government, the message of nationalism, a heightened westernization, banking and industrial skills, different accents and dialects. After such mixing and homogenizing, China's west was sure to be bound more tightly into the mainstream activities of the country, just as it was certain to lose many of its interesting and endearing localisms.

.   .   .

When I arrived at Ichang, I was out of the gorges. I learned from Miss Elsie Riebe of the American Church Mission that the city had been bombed just two days earlier, its tenth raid. The Japanese, having taken Nanking and the lower Yangtze in the preceding winter, had by the end of the summer of '38 consolidated their hold on key points between Tientsin in the north and Nanking in east-central China. The road was cleared for a move up the Yangtze to the congested tri-city area of Hankow-Wuchang-Hanyang. If that great urban complex fell, and there was scant reason to assume that it would not, Ichang could be taken by the Japanese at their ease. In which case Miss Riebe, an American citizen on American property, might, and did, play a crucial role in offering sanctuary to many Chinese, particularly women hysterically trying to avoid being victimized by Japanese soldiers.

Ichang was another cruel spot for the war's refugees. The mountain barrier which prevented the Japanese army from going west of that city, also blocked many refugees. Of the thousands who had fled there in advance of the Japanese only a fraction were able to secure river passage upstream to Free China.

.   .   .

I arranged to change ships and take passage on the British riverboat the *SS Changsha*. In first class, where I was the only passenger, I found that my lifestyle had suddenly escalated to that of a character in Somerset Maugham, for I now enjoyed clean bed linen, read *The Possessed*, and had meals with the captain. It made me feel guilty. British river vessels of that era would not sell first-class tickets to Chinese, nor sell anything but

Shih Pao Chai: Buddhist center.

On our craft right down the middle of the mighty Yangtze. We were plunging eastward through the central mountain belt, a rough region of precipitous slopes sometimes reaching ten thousand feet. It was generally scattered over three provinces—
Shansi, eastern Szechuan, and southwestern Hupei—and served as a grand divider of
north from south. Typically, north of the central mountain belt was the world of dry
plateau cultivation, the loess highlands, horse and camel transport, wheat, millet, kaoliang. South of it lay the world of Hunan and its rice cultivation, of bamboo, tea, water buffaloes, and coolie transport.

For the upstream transit, junks hugged the shore where the current was weakest. A towpath for trackers is visible. Cliffs sometimes went up two thousand feet. Upstream from Ichang to Chungking, through the central mountain belt, is one of the longest four hundred miles in the world.

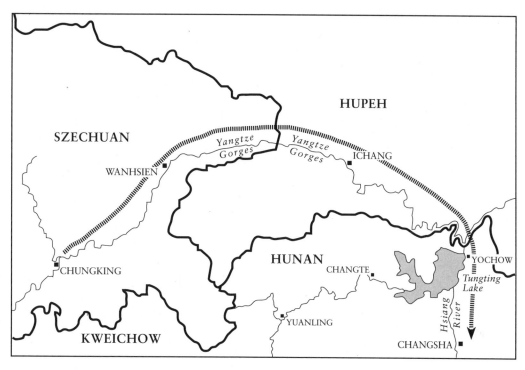

Yangtze Gorges

first class to foreigners. Having attached myself to a Chinese family which happened to be traveling, as I was, from Omei to Changsha, I was galled over the ticket and the separation. The father, registrar of one of the Chinese universities, was a man of cultural attainments and great politeness, a returned student from France and an important lawyer. He and his family had to go to a crowded, filthy area of the ship, while I was alone in colonial splendor with the captain.

At the point where the outlet from Tung Ting Lake joins the Yangtze, I went off at twilight by sampan to Yochow, another river city still in Free China but soon to fall to the Japanese. Somber thoughts about the war in abeyance, I lay on my back at the bow, watching the stars and the new moon, and enjoying the cool of the evening. A perfect hour, among the loveliest of the whole summer.

I suppose it sounds ridiculous to say that I had spent the summer learning anew that the earth is round. But in a basic sense that was true. I was now keenly aware of a part of Southeast Asia as well as of a key

171

section of West China. These were no longer abstractions to me, but important areas with living cultures, copious problems, and flesh-and-blood people. I could now see them with a sense of proportion that enabled me to assign them in my mind their rightful position on the face of the globe. Not only that, they had sufficiently impressed me with their reality that I could stand there and look with new eyes at my own country and culture, all with better awareness of both its virtues and rough edges.

In later years I often noticed that friends and acquaintances in the West rarely took Chinese or Indian or Southeast Asian culture with real seriousness. Serious music, to them, meant Mozart or Beethoven, almost never Chinese opera or Indian sitar compositions. They had not internalized Columbus's risky speculation about roundness. Nor yet today have any of our best newspapers. The *New York Times* routinely — and inexcusably — pays vastly more attention to Israel (population 4 million) than to India and China together (populations respectively approaching and exceeding 1 billion).

Matching those mental deficiencies of others was my own colossal misjudgment of the political and social fragmentation that I saw everywhere around me in the relaxed, impoverished, talkative, smiling, disorganized, polite, politically inept, war-beset scene, and that I assumed to be an inevitable characteristic of China's future. There was no room in that view for a totalitarian police state within less than fifteen years. Out of the question.

I arrived at Changsha before 10 p.m. without an air raid, finding my friends safe and in good spirits. It was almost the end of August 1938. I learned that the half-dozen air raids during my absence, one of them very bad, had caused thousands of residents to leave the city. Now, shops routinely closed during the midday hours, and many workers, refusing day work, were available only in the relative safety of the night.

The Move to Yuanling:
Autumn 1938

In Changsha, on Friday, September 2, 1938, the Senior School opened at 4:30 in the afternoon — and closed next day at 7 a.m., for the shortest term on record. The opening had been based on the decision to keep the Senior School in Changsha and send the Junior to Yuanling; later, if need be, the Senior School would move there too. Yuanling, an inconspicuous town in a rural setting, was deemed of little military interest to the Japanese and beyond their probable penetration. Hence, relatively safe. No less a figure than the governor of the province, responding to protests of parents, requested Yali to move its whole operation. Thus the sudden closing. The governor, an unpopular official from Anhwei province who had surrounded himself in Hunan with Anhwei associates, here performed one of his few popular acts.

Burton, Dwight, and two students made the two-hundred mile trip by bicycle in five days, four of them in level country, the last among heart-break hills. Most of the nights were spent with missionaries; the fourth, in a small, hilltown inn. Dwight, the one who was most athletic, had a bike with an axle problem and was very tired. I came to Yuanling on the Bank of China bus with the athletic instructor, an office assistant, a small group of students, and baggage piled to the ceiling, a cargo which threatened to shift and crush us at every curve. The ride was uncomfortable but not unpleasant. Occasional stops allowed us to stretch, and at Changte, our chief overnight stop, we were received most hospitably at

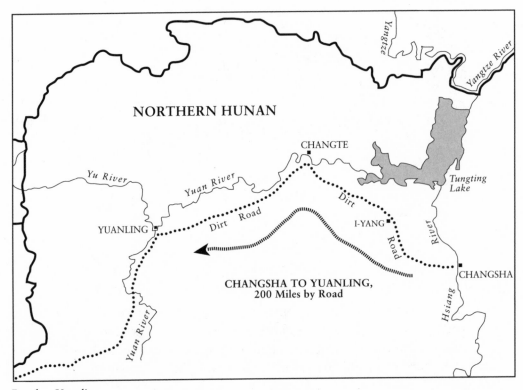

NORTHERN HUNAN

CHANGTE

Yu River

Yuan River

Tungting Lake

Dirt

Dirt Road

YUANLING

I-YANG

Road

River

CHANGSHA

CHANGSHA TO YUANLING,
200 Miles by Road

Yuan River

Hsiang

River

Yangtze

Yangtze River

Road to Yuanling

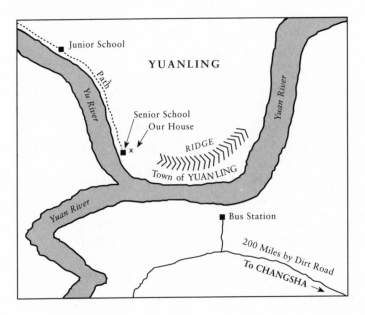

Junior School

YUANLING

Yu River

Path

Yuan River

Senior School
Our House

×

RIDGE

Town of YUANLING

Yuan River

Bus Station

200 Miles by Dirt Road

To CHANGSHA

Town of Yuanling

the bank, where our host insisted on putting us up and treating us to an evening feast. We had another morning in the bus on a winding, dusty road — one of the few automobile roads in the province — and arrived at the Yuanling bus station early in the afternoon, ready to cross the river.

We stacked our baggage in large sampans for the upstream transit. Our first view of the town was linear, and from the middle-distance it looked dirty and authentic. The sharp curve of the river was paralleled by a long curving ridge, leaving a mile of waterfront for the town itself. There was one main street, also parallel to the sandwiching constraints of hill and water. The town, although over a mile long, was thus oddly thin, and in most places extended no more than two-hundred yards back from the water.

We and our baggage came along the town waterfront close to the north bank of the river, past some handsome junks and cormorant

Our bus group en route to Yuanling; the road abnormally wide at this point. Dirt roads suitable for automobiles were just being introduced into the tumbled hill country of Central China in the 1930s. With abundant rainfall, no steel culverts, and no grading equipment, road building was reduced to contour engineering and a reliance on a clever combination of curves and gradients.

With soap rare and expensive, the family wash, done without it, took a lot of energy. It was soaked, pummeled by hand, and often beaten with a stick about the size of a billy club. A convenient spot like this, where the stones were either large, flat, and walkable, or small, smooth, and walkable, and where the water was shallow, clean, and safe, was apt to present a scene of considerable animation.

fishermen, and within earshot of the rapid patois of housewives or servants doing the family wash, soapless and by paddle. With the river low at that season, our sampans ground onto the river's rubbly edge, and we scrambled ashore. Before us, to cope with the occasional high water, there was the usual riverine flight of stone stairs—Chungking in miniature.

As we went up the steps with our luggage we wondered what lay beyond. What kind of physical setting? How cramped? How secure? How conducive to schooling? With what kind of year of teaching and learning ahead of us?

At the top of the steps we were at the west end of the town's principal street; just a few paces east was the gatehouse for the Evangelical Mission of Yuanling. Stepping through its gate, we found ourselves on our new campus, tiny, walled in the usual manner, steeply sloped.

I don't think there were any firecrackers for that arrival, but it was a special moment worthy of celebration.

Jackson Ho, Yali's athletic director, wrestling with the baggage.

Part of our group leaving by sampan from a point near the Yuanling bus station on the south bank of the Yuan River — for the last mile of our trip, across and upstream.

As unprepossessing as could be, the town revealed itself as shoulder-to-shoulder houses framed with wood, sometimes with masonry, and topped with gray tiles.

We hugged the curving north bank as we inched our way upstream, the town on our starboard.

Low water over a rocky, gravelly bottom enabled our ferryman to pole us along parallel to the north bank.

Arrival achieved. The last hundred yards of our two-hundred mile shift of campuses. If our arrival were to be symbolized by one picture, this would be it.

The house, furnished with the essentials of beds, dining room table, washstands and water pitchers, desks and screens, was maintained by two willing servants, a cook and a houseboy, both from Changsha. It was never homelike yet we asked of it just the basics, and were grateful for its space, its relative quiet, old-fashioned veranda, and liberating vista. The shortest of walks uphill before breakfast offered sunrises in gold over ranks of purple hills.

We often ate our suppers on the porch, where, so steep was the hillside, we looked over rooftops to the junction of the North Branch from Szechuan and the Yuan itself from Kweichow; thence across the omnipresent tumble of South China hills toward a distant and nearly unbroken, mountainous ridge, backed by the sunset. Upstream rain sometimes made the Yuan muddy, but the North Branch remained clear with a distinct line which persisted for several hundred yards between the two from the confluence downstream. Our vista did not warn us of the approach of storms, which came from the northeast, to our rear, but a rise of the wind accompanied by a drop in temperature usually meant we were in for rain, sometimes a severe storm.

Shou Ssu-fu, the cook, was a lively and attractive man, whose mastery of American cuisine — preferred by Burton, who was in charge of the household — came from careful training in the Changsha home of George and Erma Helde of the International YMCA. Such an apprenticeship always involved crucial sanitary procedures as well as the cooking itself. Our water was carried up from the river by water coolies and stored in an enormous earthenware jar outside the kitchen. Shou Ssu-fu daily put a pinch of alum into it to clear the mud. Since intestinal maladies lurked everywhere, we had to be careful to use the water only after boiling. We had no electricity, no central heating, no tub, and had to walk anywhere we wanted to go. Moreover, for awhile we were much isolated, a situation made worse by the Japanese decision to take Canton and cut off China's supplies from the south. Mails were tangled for weeks with virtually no foreign mail getting through; and since, in the same period there was no radio at our end of town, all our news was ancient. Then on October 17, in one glorious mail there descended letters from home dated September 3, 10, and 17 with a hoard of clippings and cartoons and masses of information.

After that miracle no mail for months.

Despite the deprivations of life in Yuanling, it was generally a very happy time. My chest of books had arrived safely ahead of me. Our household—Dwight, Burton, Fritz Schoyer (later), and myself—was eminently congenial. We were working hard at jobs we believed in, we felt needed and useful, we had exercise and shelter, food, conversation, and friendship. Whereas in the previous spring I had felt overworked, pinned down, and often miserable, I now felt open to happiness, able to recognize it and savor it.

Part of the Catholic Mission (center) in Yuanling, a mile down river from Yali. The town was long and thin, its width being only a few hundred yards from water's edge back to where I stood when I took the picture. On the far side of the river, the hills in the middle distance and the mountains back of them virtually duplicate the view from our verandah, upriver at the Yali campus.

Neighbors

Students and faculties were convinced that the Japanese invaders were particularly suspicious of intellectuals because of the latters' potential for anti-Japanese leadership, so a host of colleges and universities were moving, had already moved, or were soon to move, always with the intent of evading Japanese occupation and staying in Free China. The moves were made in a great variety of ways. One of the North China universities went to West China on foot, making a serious attempt to hold classes as faculty and students walked together the several hundred miles.

There was always the possibility that a first move might prove unworkable as the Japanese themselves penetrated the interior, and that a second move might prove necessary. No sooner had Yali and Fu Hsiang Girls' School moved from Changsha to Yuanling than each was gripped with uncertainty over the adequacy of the move, each full of rumor and speculation about a second move to Tungjen over the line in Kweichow province. By November both schools had decided to make the shift, but those decisions were cancelled in December, when the bus service to Tungjen was discontinued after eight of its buses had been stopped and robbed by bandits. A second move not only would have been unsettling, but it oddly risked going too far away from the excitement of the main population centers.

By shifting to Yuanling we expected between 100 and 200 students; by mid-September about 130 had arrived. There were accommodations for only 100, so new construction was being pushed ahead as rapidly as possible, the sawyers working before our eyes to create the boards that on the next day were nailed into place. The opening of school was postponed a week when it was clear that classroom space and equipment were inadequate.

Dining room space was so limited that there were three sittings of students and one of faculty at each meal. In the absence of chairs, diners ate standing; in the absence of beds, students slept on the floor; in the absence of a suitable hall, students stood during school assemblies. In the absence of adequate light for evening study for the younger students, I was drafted to give talks in English that were translated as I went along by one of the faculty members, either Kung Te-ta or Jackson Ho — thereby giving the students practice in their foreign language and, I hoped, supplying some fun in hearing about nonacademic subjects. I hastily put together talks on my hobbies of birds and spiders, my own prep school (Andover), railroads in the States, and bullfighting, this last based on a recent reading of Hemingway's *Death in the Afternoon*, enriched by the ardor of one of my classmates at Yale.

My own contribution was modest enough; but, enthusiastically given, it was part of a larger cooperative whole that worked like magic. Not only was Yali's survival a revelation in the applied essentials of running a school in a matchbox, but the eagerness of students and their lively morale were among the educational wonders of that era. Before the move, one would never have dared guess that we were in for a thrilling year of education.

Sawyers speedily and expertly cut the boards and beams for our new classroom building.

Between classes

Our campus was steeply sloped and held together by stone stairs; gate house in rear, the gate itself to the left of it; Main Street just beyond.

Opposite bottom: Our first school assembly on one of the few level areas of the Senior School campus, some faculty members and guests at upper left. Dr. Frank of the Evangelical Mission visible in light suit and necktie. Our treasurer, geographer and dean, left to right, face the student body. Party flag, national flag, Sun Yat Sen portrait, and under him a copy of his will.

This member of the staff was our bureaucracy — acting as office manager, registrar, and secretary to Principal Lao and Dean Ying. His desk top has both an ink bottle and the traditional inkstone and inkstick with tiny bowl of water for washing his brush-pen and for rubbing up new ink. Observe paper windows, bare walls of new lumber, and the irreducible simplicity of office equipment.

Academic industry on an extemporized desk

.   .   .

Athletic facilities at the small, crowded school compound were non-existent, so the physical education program, minimal by American standards to begin with, was reduced to walking and swimming. My own zeal for exercise and my fondness for Jackson Ho, the relaxed and witty athletic instructor, led me to explore the town and countryside with Jackson and his classes. We would pick a modest objective and walk to it, talking and taking pleasure in what there was to be seen. Often the exchanges were in English, especially with ninth grade and up. Yuanling's weather that autumn was usually clear and temperate, the hills offered relatively unobstructed walking, there were well worn public paths beside the river, the leaves of the sandalwood trees were a brilliant red, and these engaging excursions gradually acquainted us with our new home.

.　　　.　　　.

We were well away from the population centers of the province, distanced from wealth, ease of transportation, cultural excitement, and grand public buildings. Western Hunan was totally remote from the walls of the Forbidden City and the exquisite sequences of courtyards of the well-to-do in Peiping. Our town, Yuanling, oddly sinuous in shape, was drab and unkempt. It possessed an old Buddhist temple with large images, top-heavy in sculptural design to someone entering the temple, but well proportioned from the perspective of a kneeling worshipper. Tradition held that Wang An-shih, poet, chief councilor to the Emperor, and grand reformer of the eleventh century, had resided at this temple. We were cautiously informed by the Chinese equivalent of the grapevine that the temple at some point in 1938–39 had also become the special residence of Chang Hsueh-liang, one of the insurgent officers who had held and bargained with the Generalissimo in the crucial Sian Captivity of 1936 (see p. 89). He had then, according to my information, become commander of the soft underbelly of the Shanghai front in 1937 whose actions paved the way for the Japanese subversion of Shanghai and seizure of Nanking. Word had it that Chang Hsueh-liang had been placed under house arrest by the Generalissimo and held in a series of localities, one of them being our unprepossessing town.

I never saw a South China town wall in good repair. Ours was no exception. The town still had gates which could be closed, inhibiting entrance to its main street, but portions of the wall away from the street and up the hillside often suffered from advanced decrepitude. The wall appeared to give some comfort despite its decay. I recall the eerie experience of walking along the main street in the daytime with most of the shop fronts boarded up and the town's gates closed. The cobblestone street was virtually deserted except for some of the town's underfed and unloved dogs. I learned that the town feared the imminent arrival of one of the small-time warlords of our hinterland who had never been overcome by or incorporated into the central government of distant Nanking.

Later I witnessed the arrival of that bandit and his bodyguard, all in bedraggled, patched, and soiled uniforms, most of them on foot, a few being pulled in old rickshaws, guns and ammunition much in evidence, as unsmilingly watchful and tough-looking a bunch as imaginable. These roughnecks were the small fry of the shallows at one end of the warlord pool. They probably shook down the town fathers for money and then left. The following day the shops were open for business as usual.

Behind the temple and away from the river, the town abruptly yielded to the basic hills of Hunan — relatively uniform in height, deforested, the upper parts covered with grass and unkempt gravesites with their anonymous bones, the lower parts often with several levels of rice paddies. The general topography — with its ridges, steep hillsides, and narrow valleys — was much like parts of Appalachia. The mists confirmed this impression, as did the general absence of roads and the reliance on paths.

Peasant cottages with hard mud walls, wooden rooftrees and rice thatch, were dotted about. Villages were scarce, and the countryside appeared poor but was obviously not destitute. Typically, where people

"Portions of the wall . . . often suffered from advanced decrepitude."

lived there was intense cultivation — of rice, vegetables, and fish in small farm ponds. In the many localities where people did not live, there seemed virtually no attempt to utilize the land — no mixed farming, no orchard cultivation, no timber. I found this astonishing in a land of such marked population problems. However, the region must have been less poor than the immediate environs of Yuanling implied, because the markets were well-supplied with good-looking vegetables, pork and poultry, melons, pumelos, and persimmons, all of which had to come from somewhere, and that somewhere had to be within reach of our river traffic or coolies' carrying sticks.

Among the limited but special adornments of our immediate environs were the rice paddies, ever changing in color and texture, impressive in the engineering of their construction, the skill of their water management and traditional husbandry. Another special attraction was the Appalachian mist on that hill country, giving us virtually everyday the watercolor effect which turned the hills gray, poster-flat, and floating weightlessly above the earth.

Typical of the countryside just back of the ridge behind our Senior School — treeless, grassy land with stepping-stone rice paddies in the valley bottom, hills roughly uniform in height, nearby pillbox, gray horizon.

Opposite: Tobacco pipe and apparent contentment in foreground, cormorant fishing fleet in background.

Environs: Upriver from both Senior and Junior Schools — steep grassy hillsides, generally treeless, eroded, and oddly devoid of any attempts at mixed farming with animals, orchards, or woodlots.

The Move to Yuanling: Autumn 1938

Insiderness/Outsiderness

In that happy autumn in Yuanling, there were many things going on, some of them inside me, and some of those quite important, although none was properly identified nor adequately dealt with. To be a foreigner in Central China, as I was in 1938, had its full share of rewards and frustrations, many related to our particular mode and degree of insiderness/outsiderness.

We at Yali were insiders in a number of important ways. We were employed in genuinely useful jobs in a good school, which was Chinese-speaking, run by Chinese, staffed by Chinese, and attended exclusively by Chinese students. We had meaningful encounters in the classroom and abundant, friendly contacts with students, administrators, and faculty outside the classroom. So many Chinese middle school and university graduates spoke English with flair and fluency in that period that the language barrier was surprisingly minimal. We could move about with great freedom, subject only to the constraints of leg power and available transportation.

And yet, an English teacher, even with the best intentions and an absorbing curiosity about everything Chinese, was inevitably an outsider. A cultural gap existed: the Chinese family was a unit unto itself; there was no easy, American-style tradition of inviting friends in for dinner, and the straitened circumstances of wartime simply enhanced these barriers.

I would gladly have read anything on China, but little was available to a foreigner who read only beginner's Chinese. This lack was only partly a function of the war situation; it was chiefly due to the substantial and ridiculous nonawareness of China by American newspapers, journals, writers, scholars, teachers, and publishers in the period when I was at school and college. America, still in the era of missionary hagiography and Pearl Buck, was only barely entering the present era of scholarly scrutiny and penetrating journalism.

My reading therefore took what form it could. I found a copy of Reichelt's *Truth and Tradition in Chinese Buddhism*, where the author offered basic and sensitive insights into Buddhist theology and organization. He argued that the identifiable common ground between Christianity and Buddhism could serve as a creative point of contact between East and West; and he founded a religious retreat in Kowloon to that end. I found Soothill's translation of *The Lotus of the Wonderful Law*, a tenth-century text; Legge's nineteenth-century translation of the Confucian classics was available, as were copies of the long, episodic Chinese novels *All Men are Brothers*, *The Romance of the Three Kingdoms*, and *The Dream of the Red Chamber*. All of these I devoured. But then what for a compulsive reader? I fell back on the occidental poetry and novels that I had taken with me and on what could be found on the bookshelves of friends — oddly my first reading of *Alice in Wonderland*; then the great translations of Proust by Scott-Moncreiff and of *The Tale of Genji* by Arthur Waley — for me pure enchantment; Shakespeare's *Sonnets*; works by Joyce, Sophocles, Dostoevski, Edmund Wilson, T. S. Eliot, Conrad, and James Jeans. Heady stuff, all of it, but hardly literary keys opening the way to a fuller identification with China.

I had more reason to be sensitive to this problem in my second year — during the first I was busy getting into the swing of things, whereas during the second I was much more alive to what was accessible to a foreigner and what was not and never would be.

I don't recall that we ever discussed the disadvantages of our outsiderness, or even regarded it as something to be identified and commented on. I'm sure it would have helped me to have talked it out, a process which might have taken place if our Senior Bachelors had remained in China beyond the middle of that first school year, or if we had not lost Ruth Greene and George Helde in the general exodus. Those two, experienced and wise and sensitive, were well-equipped to help us over this hurdle.

My feelings were related to the previous summer's search for the essential China, and were complicated by a devastating perfectionist impulse. I did not know how to recognize that I had achieved a lot, enough to be happy about — and, at the same time, reconcile it with the realization that I would inevitably remain an outsider. It was not a problem of alienation, but one of the alien outsider. Had I been a Chinese detesting my own Chinese culture and trying to drop out, that would have been alienation. I was, on the other hand, an alien standing on the outside looking in, enamored of what I saw, yet unable really to be a part of it.

I suppose it was foolish to be upset by this when so much else was going well. Inevitably outside the walls of Chinese family life, any foreigner — no matter how talented or well-trained — was doomed to be an observer and a bystander. Moreover, in a profound sense, who in China did not have outsiderness to cope with? Even the Chinese scholar, for all his essential Chineseness, was an alien in language and custom in most of his own Chinese world, since 80 percent or more of his country's population were peasants inhabiting a village world whose mores, dialects, and rhythms were usually so totally at variance with his own that the scholar could easily be as out of context as a camel in a rice paddy.

Whatever the problem and its overtones, I did feel the outsiderness, often acutely, and had no solution to it.

Graduation picture of the fourteenth senior class of Yali Middle School, May 1939 (the twenty-eighth year of the Republic of China). Taken in front of the Lower School outside Yuanling.

The School in Yuanling

The figures in the front row of the photograph on p. 198 were the men who staffed the school during the first refugee year in Yuanling. Talkative and lively the minute before, they here present themselves under the momentary tyranny of the camera lens in their least characteristic role — as Inscrutable Orientals. This was the group who had brought their families to Yuanling to be sheltered in hopelessly cramped quarters wherever rooms were available. Some were undergoing private miseries — the breakdown of a wife in the case of Lo Hwei-lin, or for Jackson, the deafness from birth of two of his children. As salaried middle-class teachers, all were feeling the pinch of inflation. Their Nationalist currency was being overprinted and poured into the economy without adequate backing, and with predictable results. As one small index of trouble, their dollar — relative to the American dollar — had slipped in the course of the year from 3 : 1 to somewhere between 6 : 1 and 8 : 1. Not yet disastrous but unnerving and hinting at an even worse future.

They had the satisfactions of serving an adaptive, high-quality school and of helping train an able group of students who could be expected to go on to university work and subsequently play substantial roles in politics, business, and the professions. They seemed to me to represent a fairly restricted sector of the ideological spectrum in China of that era. As a group they accepted Sun Yat Sen's creed of nationalism, republicanism, and economic development. That meant, further, that they went

199

along with Sun's general scheme of a military ordering of China's warlord chaos under the temporary dictatorship of the Kuomintang with a hoped-for subsequent advance into democracy.

Such would have been the general framework of their politics up to 1937. They had committed themselves to support of Chiang Kai-shek during the period of the latter's most creative leadership—from 1927 to 1938. Their political philosophy had been brutally affirmed by the Japanese invasion of China. Conventionally and strongly anti-Japanese, this faculty group was prepared to subordinate everything to the war effort and had chosen, with hardly a second thought, to move with the school and stay in Free China. Only one of their colleagues was sufficiently stirred by word from the new Communist area of the northwest to leave the school and join the Communists. Some of these men were Christians; none Moslem; none Buddhist. All, in varying degrees, were a part of the disintegrating Confucian tradition of the scholar gentleman: elitist, moral, low-key, middle-of-the-road, patriotic, believing in a homogenized core of Chinese culture with a basic political unity to the country. They seemed to me rarely boisterous, never reckless, and to possess an acute sense of limits; not glacially self-contained like a Navajo, but smilingly accessible to friendship and yet shy of intimacy; unsentimental, quietly courageous, with no interest in an ostentatiously noble pose.

They possessed the endless Chinese capacity to observe candidly, to accommodate, to give and yet retain. In a modern setting they represented the bamboo resiliency of the Confucian scholar-gentleman.

.   .   .

My eyes were used hard. I read a lot in my free time, and I had student papers to correct. Both of these activities often took place in poor light from kerosene lamps. Other factors, such as vitamin deficiency and wartime stress, may have contributed to persistent eye discomfort. Overcoming an obstacle sometimes lifts one to a higher plateau; that happened to me without my realizing at the time what I was doing. To compensate for my inability to read more than an irreducible minimum, I began to spend more time with the Chinese members of the faculty and took to socializing in the office and faculty room where several members of the staff could usually be found, tea glasses in hand, seated around the charcoal fire. We all wore sufficient clothes to keep reasonably warm whether indoors or out, adding only scarf and hat for the latter. That still allowed hands and feet to get miserably cold, a condition worse for the Chinese in their black cloth shoes. The cold was beautifully dealt with by a seat at the fire, feet up on the low wooden fender that held the brazier, hands nursing a glass of green tea or held out over the embers. Never in my experience had a fire no larger than a saucer been so thoroughly and pleasingly utilized. I liked the characteristic spent smell of charcoal. I enjoyed the flow of good-humored conversation, sometimes in Chinese, often in English. Those men made it easy for me to forget my outsiderness and feel comfortable with them. Learning to enjoy doing less and to look more deeply into the nature of everyday things, I became less of an intellectual and more of a person.

Mr. Wang, our good-humored and lively geographer, was one of the regulars of the faculty room, as was Mr. Shao, teacher of the Chinese classics, who had me buy small samples of many kinds of green tea, and

Mr. Wang, genial geographer

Mr. Shao, Confucian classicist

then came up to our house to help me distinguish their characteristics and react to them. For these men, particularly the latter, Confucianism was still a living reality. To Mr. Shao philosophy would have seemed less a Teutonic pyramid of systematic ideas, abstract and unrelated to daily life, than a code of conduct, rules of thumb, aphorisms, and working platitudes. Chinese society, he would have held, could still draw its strength from these Confucian roots. Our Christian witness found its parallel in his Confucian witness.

· · · ·

Our students were to experience the war years rather differently than did their faculty. Teenagers, they were yet unencumbered by full family responsibilities. Their education still in process, they were shaped as young adults more by the war years than by the prewar thirties. That was an important difference because their chief exposure to the Kuomintang government came after it had lost its national capital at Nanking, was under desperate pressures, and in retreat to West China. The collapse of the Kuomintang for China Proper was a decade away. When it came, it appeared to me to be more the product of the terrible burden of the war than anything else, but that burden was already evident by 1938 in a host of different ways such as the flood of refugees, inflation, war casualties, and bombing destruction. The political exposure of our students was fraught with war tensions and disappointments, and this group was less hopeful than its immediate predecessors.

These students and the Chinese staff had already narrowed their options by electing to go with the school, remain in Free China, and continue their education. Some of their classmates of the previous year had remained in Changsha, accepting the likelihood of coming under Japanese occupation. A few had dropped out of school and enlisted in the Nationalist Army in defiance of the government's preference that they complete their education, since trained personnel was in short supply. One had dropped out to try to join Mao Tze-tung, Chu Teh, and the Eighth Route Army some hundreds of miles away in their new location in the northwest.

Our students, winnowed in these ways by the changing circumstances of the war, shared a fixity of purpose that helped enormously to carry the school through its adjustments to education in Yuanling. The students' commitment to education meant that school was more meaningful, morale higher, and classes easier to teach. Their class ties were strong, both in the sense of social class and school class; their family units were decisive, the family being thought of as not only extended in the contemporary scene, but back over the centuries to their ancestors and forward to their unborn descendants; they wrote their fathers in dehydrated classical Chinese; they bowed simultaneously every Monday morning to the portrait of Sun Yat Sen; Confucius was still sacred writ, despite the multiple crumblings of the old society. They had clearly been brought up without any British cherishing of social eccentrics. In these and other ways they hung together like bats in a tower.

Nevertheless, they thought of themselves as highly individualistic, as they indeed were in important respects. They had chosen not only to devote themselves to their education, but to a westernized form of it. They were religiously eclectic and tolerant. They were free to express diverse opinions on a great variety of subjects; they were keeping a variety of choices open for careers in business, government, or the

A very conscientious and able student, one of those whose school bills could no longer be met by parents after catastrophic family losses in the war. Photograph taken on the verandah of our house, just above the Senior School. He and others used the verandah as an office for editing a school paper in English.

professions. They were free to move about, subject only to pocketbooks, the war, and their vacation time. Given the constraints and pressures that channel all nations through phases of sameness in time of war, the homogeneity was neither excessive nor oppressive in 1938–39.

.   .   .

The Senior School (ages sixteen to eighteen) was housed in a one-acre, walled compound on a steep hillside, with gatehouse on the lower side, kitchen and dining room adjacent, then — partway up the slope — the smallest administrative office in the history of educational bureaucracy, two hastily built classroom structures, Dwight's tiny office, and finally several modified-Victorian, faculty residences at the top. The slope must have been close to forty-five degrees. The six classrooms had the simplest furnishings imaginable for about twenty students apiece — small table for the teacher, benches and writing surfaces for the students, unfinished wooden walls, windows glazed with paper, and no heating arrangements. For this a student paid fees between $100 and $150 Mex (about $25 U.S. in Yuanling at that time) for one semester at Yali. Thus, for $50 U.S. I was able to finance an entire school year for one of my best pupils, whose family property had been destroyed.

There were no electives, and the students spent the day in their homerooms as the teachers shifted about. Utterly simple as these arrangements were, they were entirely adequate for the English Department which had never relied on anything more elaborate than textbooks-and-teacher. For someone like Lo Hwei-lin of the Science Department, teaching with minimal equipment must have been exceedingly frustrating. He managed somehow and kept his smile despite this deprivation and the more serious problem of his wife's terrible bout with mental illness.

The ten-minute break between classes, giving us all a chance to move about, was a lovely interlude. Nothing much happened, but there was bustle, reading of bulletin boards, and a certain flow of wit and laughter. When the cold weather established itself in classrooms, recesses offered a blessed chance to restore one's circulation.

School, more informal and more intimate than before, went well. The Chinese, more than any other society that I know, have mastered congestion; they are expert at using codes of politeness as a very practical way

205

Between classes: Jackson Ho, inseparable from his felt hat, chatting with students in the Senior School. This was one of the new buildings in our hillside compound.

of softening human abrasiveness and enabling large numbers of people to live together without irreparably getting on each other's nerves. I saw these dynamics in action in Yuanling, largely on the part of young Chinese, and was impressed by their performance and its social workability.

Our microcosm suggested to me that Chinese society canonized the practical and the workable; it seemed dedicated to getting results with minimal effort, the least fuss, and at little expense; it maximized family relations and obligations, and minimized the individual. It appeared to me to discourage individual flamboyance, and utilize, as social lubricants, both politeness and humor.

.   .   .

During the first period each Monday morning (8:30 to 9:30) there was a Sun Yat Sen memorial assembly just as there had been in Changsha. For lack of a hall, the Yuanling version continued to be an out-of-doors affair, the well-ventilated audience standing in the courtyard of rented property on the river side of North Main Street, just across from the Senior School. Headmaster Lao turned toward the poster portrait of Sun Yat Sen, and recited, as in schools all over Nationalist China at that hour, the Will of Dr. Sun, one of the key parts of the Kuomintang creed. "I have devoted forty years to the work of the Nationalist Revolution, . . ." My mind wandered from the earnest message of that failed physician and frustrated revolutionary to the suavity of Mr. Lao's cadenced delivery. ". . . we must wake up the masses of the country and unite with those races of the world who . . ." Moss gathering again, I might wonder how it was ever decided to use someone's will in this way. Had George Washington left any such message for me in his will? His Farewell Address, yes; there he told me to avoid entangling alliances. But his will?? Was this incantation some kind of clue about Chinese mores that eluded me? ". . . the three Principles of the People written by me, and the Declaration of the. . . ." Mr. Lao raced on, his face revealing nothing, his voice metronomic and clear, the tones Hunanese and accented. "The calling of the People's Congress and the abolition of the unequal treaties . . . must be realized within the shortest possible time. This is what I wish to call to your attention." Ending, he and the entire gathering bowed three times to the portrait, deeply, from the waist, hands at sides. Had this taken place in 1900 instead of 1938 the assembly, all with loyalty queues, would have knelt and bowed nine times before a portrait of the Empress Tzu-hsi. 1938 republicanism, streamlining that operation, had removed the queue and the awe, and substituted filial respect. Continuity had been modified, but not thrown away.

Discontinuity was accented when Dwight stepped forward and led the choir of eight or ten Christian boys in a hymn. The assembly, only a minority of which were Christians, stood politely. After a few announcements from Dean Ying, either he or Mr. Lao usually gave a talk calculated to train, assist, and exhort the teenagers before him.

It was all quite painless except that Chinese propensities to volubility often took advantage of such an orderly captive audience. We could, however, count on being saved by the bell — in this case, the one for the

Dwight leading the choir. Mr. Lao seated at right, students, many of them in scout uniform, standing.

beginning of second period classes. Public meetings, on the other hand, could tax an audience much more severely, as illustrated by the Peiping story about the young replacement for an august retiring member of the British Diplomatic Corps. The latter, obviously a veteran of many a long-winded public address by Chinese orators was asked for sage advice before his departure. His counsel to his youthful replacement: "Take a pee whenever you get the chance."

.   .   .

Boy Scouts continued in Yuanling as a regular part of school activity. Scout uniforms were often worn to class; the patriotic, self-reliant and paramilitary aspects of scouting fitted easily into the wartime aspirations and needs of the Nationalist government.

Scouting also lent itself to the day trip, which had entered our curriculum. About once a week each class got out for a holiday jaunt to one of the nearby mountains or towns. On a sunny, autumnal Saturday I joined Jackson Ho and one of his classes in a foray into the countryside of Yuan Tai Shan. After a hike of several miles, Jackson split the class into two parts and sent them up different hills, the idea being to carry out some weighty communication in English by semaphore. The scouts, good at intermediate English, had a great time watching the other hillside, calling out the letters as they were signaled. Someone wrote them down, and the group took a hand at making sense of the message. Our answer was written out and slowly semaphored back. I remembered my own scouting in New England well enough to be able to participate. It was great fun. By adding Chinese talkativeness, vivacity and wit, you can get an idea of the pleasure and charm of that hilltop scene.

Later the whole group reassembled and visited a nearby Taoist temple before our return to the school. In our part of China the Taoist temples were usually unkempt and uninviting. This one was dingy and dirty; its one attendant, slovenly and dispirited. For that day at least, modernity, juxtaposed to antiquity, won all the laurels.

.   .   .

"Jackson split the class into two parts and sent them up different hills. . . . Our answer was written out and slowly semaphored back."

My years in Changsha and Yuanling were a time of developing cataclysm for China; and — for Japan — of wading yet more deeply into a morass. As of my second year at Yali, China's military position was bad but not hopeless. The Generalissimo, never a charismatic leader, nevertheless had great Face. He had dared to undertake leadership at a time that required comprehensive change and had presided over a decade of considerable creativity in which Western victimization of China had been reduced, the currency had been unified, universities expanded, roads and railroads extended, hospital facilities increased, opium to an appreciable extent suppressed, and programs in mass literacy and rural reconstruction launched. There was a long way to go, but many bold and creative steps had been taken. Evidence of the effectiveness of his leadership lay in the Japanese invasion itself largely motivated, we assume, by Japan's need to prevent the emergence of a strong, unified, and effective China.

Chiang's varied program for reform came under such great pressure from the Japanese invasion that a good deal of it was in jeopardy in 1939. The war, rather than the intrinsic shortcomings of the Kuomintang, was the chief source of his difficulties.

Whatever its shortcomings, the government during my years at Yali was generally — and fortunately — remote. We at Yali were well removed from slogans, from officialese, from bureaucrats, from government bossiness. Not only that, but as foreigners we were neither confined to cages, nor were there any cosmetics between China and us — no Potemkin villages, no tours, no guides, no prophylactic partitions, no compulsory visits to diesel factories. Our tourism-travel provided contact with full-blooded, three-dimensional people. Having nothing organized for us, we earned what we found out, utterly unlike visits to China of the 1970s and 1980s.

Fritz Schoyer (later placed in the awesome and bizarre position of being a kind of unofficial mayor of part of Shanghai for a year after the Japanese surrender in 1945, where he was thrown up against the racketeers, the pimps and prostitutes, the con men and urban sharpies of all types, the ill and the dispossessed) came to feel that he and we at Yali had been in touch with the best of modern China.

Yali was an institution that saw value in what the West had to offer in terms of friendship, Christian helpfulness, education, and training for leadership. The Union School of missions in Hunan Province, Yali had a good scattering of rural boys sent up by mission schools, but mostly students from middle- or upper middle-class families. With American financial support for its balanced westernized curriculum and specialty in language training, it had become the best school in Hunan and probably one of the best in China.

Yali kept going throughout the nightmare of the war, doing its share in training young Chinese. There was much more interruption of education by the Red Guards during the Cultural Revolution when all the schools were closed in 1966, the secondary schools for as long as four years. There was, thus, much less continuity of schooling at the hands of the Chinese Communists than during the nightmare of the Japanese invasion.

A stunning example of binational cooperation in a private institution on a person-to-person basis, Yali was preeminently an illustration of

Christian helpfulness. Although most members of the school were non-Christian and none was harried by evangelism, many could be described as "agnostics with a religious temperament," as was said of Bertrand Russell. They were sympathetic to the aims of Yali, appreciative of its many contributions, and happily participant in its special type of educational make-up.

Our River

Rivers in the interior of China in the 1930s were almost entirely without bridges. Small streams had bridges, canals had them, but not the rivers, with very few exceptions. The Yellow River, one of those exceptions, had a rickety railroad bridge that inspired so little confidence that one of the Yali doctors, whenever she crossed it, stood in the vestibule at the end of her railway car so as to have at least a fighting chance if the bridge chose that moment to collapse.

The absence of bridges was a revelation to my young American eyes. Having assumed that bridges were simply there, at appropriate places under roads, I was repeatedly and pleasantly surprised by their absence. And not only that, but by how "unnecessary" they were in the first place, since a traditional society seemed to get along well without them. The absence of bridges meant the presence of sampan ferries and the importance of their handlers, the boat people. It meant an appreciable separation of the two sides, so you would see your friends less often if a river lay between you. It meant the slowed-down pace of an earlier China, whether for goods or for passengers. It meant that I became more aware of rivers than I had ever been at home in the States—of the height of water, its movement, the play of light on it, the mists, the cormorant fishing craft, the variations in boat design. As I observed the utter simplicity of ferry technology, I had a daily glimpse into ancient China.

Water was of very evident importance, and Yuanling, possessing two modest but not inconsequential branch rivers that came together at the west end of the town, had a considerable body of water next to its entire length. With a small but growing, jerry-built suburb across the river where the road connecting Yuanling with Changte began at the bus depot, there were always plenty of people wanting to cross the river. Sampans supplied the ferry service, just as they did in thousands of other spots in South China.

The ferry service at Yuanling was straightforward and uncomplicated, since it dealt with a safe stretch of a relatively small river and had to handle only people and their baggage. Cars were not brought over from the bus station to Yuanling proper; indeed, the latter had never been visited by an automobile. On the other hand, conveying cars across a river by raft was a relatively common procedure in several parts of the province. The typical ferry landing, when one traveled by truck, car, or bus, had usually offered a bit of relaxation to the traveler. The driver drew up behind one or more predecessors, got out to stretch and watch the boatman manipulate the one-car ferry. All very slow-moving and pleasant. By 1938 this process had deteriorated into an occasion for anxiety because Japanese planes took to dropping undelivered bomb loads at these sites, strafing the cars and their scattered occupants. If ferries were well removed from towns, the travelers who clustered around them were not warned by the familiar and frightening wail of the town sirens, but had to depend on their own alertness. There was less clustering of cars and people, as it became more prudent to wait a few hundred yards away for one's turn on the ferry. This small irony of the war — the pleasure of the ferry-stop being replaced by uneasiness — found its counterpart in our fear of good weather, whether sunshine or full moon, because of air raids.

The war had its share of grand ironies too. The Japanese, intent on expanding their mainland holdings, saw in Chiang Kai-shek their greatest obstacle. Yet, the more the Japanese won, the deeper they wallowed into the bog and the closer they came to their own ultimate destruction. Moreover, one of their special motivations in entering China had been anticommunism, but their assault was chiefly directed against one of the most formidable anti-Communist leaders of the twentieth century, Chiang Kai-shek himself. As they had driven him from the eastern half of

China, robbing him of the resources of that more-developed half of his country, they had drastically weakened his regime as an anti-Communist force, opening the way for Communist survival and expansion, the very thing they dreaded.

Furthermore, although Chiang's Nationalists were ultimately victors in the war against Japan, they had been so weakened and so corrupted by the battering of the war itself that they had become hollow men who could be blown over by the Communists. In short, in the grandest irony of all, it could be argued that the anti-Communist leaders of Japan did more for the Communist cause than anyone, including the Communists themselves.

. . .

Junks, omnipresent in watery South China, were tantalizing to me. I wanted to photograph them more freely than I dared in wartime, and I wanted to know about them. They contained the microcosm of a mysterious way of life, alien from me by virtue of their being Chinese, and alien from most Chinese by being waterborne. I wondered whether these river gypsies came ashore and what they did when ashore. What was their degree of Chineseness? Did they speak the local patois or did they have a water-nomad dialect of their own? Were they wanderers or did they confine themselves to a locality defined by their language? Were they totally atomized and competitive or somehow protected by togetherness and benevolent associations? Did they typically own their own craft, maintain it, live and die in it? Or were they hirelings? Tempting questions all, yet I knew no one — whether scholar, missionary or lay citizen — who knew any of the answers.

The coastal junk — large, decked, often two-masted — was a different breed from our inland type. The latter, as seen along the Changsha waterfront, was a medium-sized, graceless craft that conveyed a sense of working, ageless toughness. A living fossil, it was one-masted with a windsock at the top, and had a square, cotton mainsail, ropes waterproofed with oil and pigs' blood, varnished camphorwood hull, and interior watertight compartments sheltered by sliding arched covers. Slow, snug, unnamed, and durable, it carried a south-pointing compass. Its sluggishness and lack of style made it seem more the craft of water

No cars had ever crossed to the town, but the ferry service moved appreciable numbers of people and goods, genially and efficiently. Simple wooden planking over the shallows served for landings and kept passengers dry shod — and alert. The gravelly beach allowed secure footing.

peasants than of mariners, yet judged by its economic viability over the millennia, I think it must be one of the all-time winners. Clipper ships, for all their grace and brilliance, their meaningfulness to a New Englander like myself, were gone after only one generation of glory — while the junk plods on.

On a Sunday in Changsha during my first year at Yali, my friend Dr. Walter Liebenthal and I were out walking the riverbank in the northwest quarter of the city. We stopped to admire a trim cluster of junks which had been moored for the night and then stepped carefully aboard via a long springy gangplank. Invited into the flagship of the flotilla, we walked along the slender gunwale catwalk just above the water to the area in the stern where the crew ate and slept. Our hosts, friendly and courteous, offered us low stools, tea, and cigarettes. Inspection revealed the junks to be spic-and-span throughout. We were informed they were Changsha's nightsoil fleet. When the city's contribution had been delivered to the rice fields, the compartments were mopped out and the boats took on a return cargo of rice, part of which we had doubtless eaten.

In this outing, we had stumbled on a part of China that was totally remote from the clichés of her chosen self-image — that of porcelain, calligraphy, ceremonial bronzes, and jade connoisseurship.

The river junks of Yuanling obviously differed greatly in design from others. Among inland models there were, of course, local differences, but junks seemed confined to a traditional, stodgy spectrum. The only exception to this in my experience were the junks of Yuanling. These vessels were substantial but slimmer than most others, and the helmsman worked from a raised stern which often had real gracefulness and elegance. It took me some time to account for the design. Not having

Yuan River junks with their distinctive sterns.

come to Yuanling by boat, a slow trip upriver from Tung Ting Lake, past Changte and Tao Hwa Leng, I didn't realize that the numerous white-water sections of the Yuan River made those high sterns protective of the helmsman and thoroughly functional.

Since the automobile road to the town was very recent, any earlier travel to or from Yuanling was apt to have been done by junk. Trips both downriver and back on one of these craft had been made, as I was soon to learn, by all the older missionaries and mission families in Yuanling. I regret never having made that voyage.

.   .   .

The Junior School was about half an hour distant, up the North Branch, transportation being by shoeleather. I taught classes at the Senior School during the first and second periods, walked the two miles to the Junior School during the third period in order to teach there in the fourth, then had lunch, sometimes taught again, and walked back to the Senior School. Outward bound the walk passed below a large hilltop building with sharply upturned corner eaves, and immediately crossed a stone bridge, where several people could usually be found selling goods displaying the characteristically minuscule capitalism that offered items like a single cigarette for a penny.

On the right, beyond the bridge stood a much smaller temple, also with radically upturned roof corners. For appreciable stretches of the walk there were stepping stones to maintain the path and allow one to escape mud in time of rain. Systematically spaced for Chinese legs, they reminded us of walking on railroad ties, too close for an American stride, and not close enough for us to fit two within one stride.

Hilltop pagodas were visible. Usually tapered and always possessing an uneven number of stories, they sought to placate the dragon in the river as insurance against drought or flood, neither condition very far from the minds of Hunanese farmers and river families. Landmarks rather than shrines, the pagodas were empty and deserted, usually unkempt and in disrepair when I saw them up close, but also winning, mysterious, and comforting.

The path hugged the river's edge, gently rising and falling in the hilly terrain. During one of my walks, at a point where I was perhaps thirty feet above the river, I could look into a kettle of dark-eared kites, about twenty of which were flying tight spirals and circles over some river refuse that fascinated them. When one dipped to snatch a bit, it immediately had to deal with the stooping attacks of the nineteen others, each ravenous for a share. I had never been so close to the beautiful and tense gyrations, the sophisticated aerial acrobatics of large birds.

Usually one encountered people carrying things. Outsized loads were often borne by apparently elderly women, their modest social status suggested both by the burdens and their unbound feet. Although foot-binding—so far as we could tell—was no longer inflicted on middle-class and upper-class girls to establish their acceptability in marriage, the accomplishment of this vast social shift was so recent that we often saw middle-aged and elderly women tottering about good-naturedly on bound feet. Peasant girls had been spared this ordeal.

There were many river scenes of great peace and beauty during these repeated midmorning and midafternoon walks and during our hikes further up the river. The water of the North Branch, in distinction to the Yuan itself, was utterly clear. Burton recalls the pleasure, after teaching at the Junior School on a very hot day, of wading out over a bar and lying down in the crystalline shallows.

The path crossed another small bridge, passing an earth-shrine and some modest peasant homes. The walk seemed to imbed me even more deeply in utterly remote, provincial countryside, then suddenly I arrived at the wooden paling which enclosed the Junior School, its group of attractive one- and two-story buildings forming a compact rectangle. Some small residences stood nearby. In traditional design with papered windows and ice-cold classrooms in the winter, the buildings were thought to have been put up for some military purpose which was then abandoned. Simple but adequate, they fell to us in mint condition, the only disadvantages being that they were perhaps too remote for high morale, and that some word may have gotten to the Japanese of the earlier military intent, making the compound a probable target.

A year or more after my walks to the Junior School, the path was used as a kind of military route in this roadless countryside, where conscripts, roped together for control, were marched toward some distant front. Thin and pathetic, they could not be visualized as ever becoming effective soldiers. If sick, they were left to die. Jeannette Lin, moving her hospital from the danger of the town to the greater security of the North Branch across from the Junior School, was able to establish a clinic for the stragglers, a thoughtful and characteristic action of that generous doctor.

Top: En route to the Junior School: surveying class — one Senior School student and seven absorbed onlookers from the general public.

En route to the Junior School: surveying class and the small bridge at the beginning of the walk. The North Branch flows toward the camera, joining the Yuan River just to the left, out of the picture.

En route to the Junior School: dilapidated temple just beyond the bridge. The scowl in the foreground was one of the inhibitions to taking pictures freely in wartime.

En route to the Junior School: upstream from the junction of the Yuan River and the North Branch. One of those mysterious clusters of junks with its specialized waterborne life, drying fishnets, adjacent towpath.

Part of the path next to our river. A small earth shrine to propitiate some local deity stands just to the left of the entrance of the structure through which the path passes. Trees were a rarity, but camphorwood, which I think this is, could be found near temples.

Top: A hamlet penned between river and grassy slopes, with shingle beach and junks — all very usual; but shaded by a grove of trees — most unusual.

On those excursions the students liked to purchase sections of sugar cane or handfuls of *liang hsu*, a root vegetable. The brown sweet potato-like husk could be split and peeled off revealing a gleaming white interior textured like an Irish potato, moist and relatively tasteless, which could be eaten raw like an apple. Closest to it among possible American counterparts would be the Jerusalem artichoke. It served as a snack or luncheon on our hikes.

Jackson was an informal, reasonably energetic, and amiable companion on these jaunts. It didn't bother him to switch back and forth between English and Chinese; he often interpreted exchanges or idioms for me without my having to ask for help. He liked to banter, and we all laughed a lot, but he was adept at retaining the Face and dignity of the teacher as well. Students felt relaxed with him but did not take advantage of his informality.

We passed through occasional hamlets where the dust, the mud walls and old rice thatch, the few rice terraces and pepper plants suggested that the economics of survival must have been exceedingly precarious. That world was as distant from my Chinese companions as from me. Its wave lengths and rhythms were different from those of Changsha and Yuanling; the patois was often unintelligible to any of us. If our students stopped to consider the few items which might be for sale, the communication, such as it was, appeared civil, neutral, dignified, devoid of either surliness or condescension.

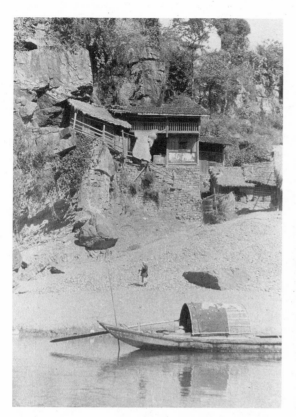 

Despite the trees, my impression was that such a spot could just as well have been lifted out of a remote rural area in China a millennium ago.

Right: Boatman from this remote world.

The Changsha Fire

My China experiences routinely veered from idyll to shock, and back again. That autumn in Yuanling was largely idyll — I loved going to bed soon after lamplight, sleeping on the upstairs screened porch, waking at dawn to the screams of a pig being slaughtered at the butcher shop below our house; falling asleep again to wake at sunrise and be able to look down on the river. The unpleasantness of the previous spring had given way to exhilaration and happiness.

Then came the devastating news via Manila Radio that Changsha had been destroyed. Our jumbled information about it slowly revealed that the city had suffered enormously from manmade fires, but that the Yali campus on the north side of the city had somehow been saved. One of our first circumstantial confirmations was from Commissioner of Education Chu, who joined us for a meal. He had visited Changsha shortly after the fire and reported that our friends there were all safe.

Since my eye trouble had begun by then, and since several attempts to see a doctor in Kweiyang had been unsuccessful, it had been decided to send me to Changsha where there was still an opthalmologist, and where I could see for myself what had happened to the city. Dr. George Tootell, an ebullient American medical missionary, was in Yuanling trying to get home to Changte, downriver from us and halfway to Changsha. He relentlessly badgered a Chinese official until the latter released gasoline for the trip in an automobile which was at the disposal of Mr. Scott, an

The river often represented all that was idyllic to me.

English official of the International Red Cross. I was invited to accompany them. We made it safely to Changte, although at one ferry crossing we were very uneasy about being bombed or strafed by Japanese planes. In Changte I stayed with the Tootells. Early each day I went to the bus station to catch the nonappearing Changsha bus—and each day returned in some embarrassment to the Tootells for an unexpected series of days amounting finally to a week's visit which included Christmas. On one of those failed days I went with Dr. Tootell to his hospital, where he put me in mask and gown to watch an operation. The patient was pathetic in the extreme—a fearful, emaciated man with a month-long, compound fracture of the leg, who came to the Western doctor only as a last resort. He tried feebly to escape from the operating room, to be rather brusquely but not unkindly dissuaded by Dr. Tootell, who was sure that amputation offered the patient his only chance. The anesthetizing, cutting, sawing, and suturing were accomplished quickly. I managed to watch it all without having to leave the operating room.

This doctor typified the hard-working, provincial medical missionary. Hale and hearty, chubby, gruff-sounding, an eminently practical man, a good manager, married to a prim, easily shocked lady from Knoxville, he was the one foreign doctor and often the only doctor, at the isolated Presbyterian hospital in a medium-sized town of western Hunan. There for years as doctor and surgeon, he had treated an immense variety of health problems.

I never knew the outcome of the amputation because my bus did indeed arrive the day following but I have often thought of that patient who so desperately needed—and dreaded—Dr. Tootell's help.

.　　.　　.

For some days before the fire rumors had circulated in Changsha that the city was to be sacrificed to deny it to the Japanese, who were then in nearby Yochow, less than fifty miles to the north. People were being urged to leave the city, and those who had relatives in the province were going to them.

Sunday evening, November 13, Phil Greene and Frank Hutchins were dinner guests at the temporary residence of Governor Chang outside the South Gate. In Phil's account, although they feasted royally and were assured by the governor that the rumors of scorched earth were entirely false, the party was suddenly sent home at 11 p.m. Frank and Phil were taken by military car in a circuitous route well east of the city in order to avoid the glut of people, most of them on foot but many utilizing cars, buses, trucks, wheelbarrows and rickshaws. When the two finally reached Yali, Phil went to bed and fast asleep, to be wakened by Frank at about 4 a.m. to see the sky bright from dozens of blazes in the city.

They discovered later that the fanatical group that had so resented the fall of Wuhan and Canton to the Japanese in late October had removed firefighting equipment from the city — generally interpreted by people as a signal to flee — and formed gangs of about ten who entered houses, threw the residents' flammables on and under the stairs, dashed kerosene on them, and touched a match to the pile.

Frank remained on the Yali campus; Phil went over to Hsiang Ya; each spent his time putting out occasional firebrands thrown over the walls and, more importantly, dissuading groups from setting fire to our buildings. As they were so occupied, rats began to pour out of the city in what became a flood so dense that it seemed to cover the ground. Doors and windows had to be tightly secured. When the flood was at its height, a period lasting about twelve hours, Phil found it difficult to get out of a door without a dozen rats squeezing in.

The Changsha fire blazed furiously for about three days, the second being the worst. As areas were burned out, follow-up gangs arrived to fire whatever was left standing. Around noon of the third day a gang of about fifteen arrived to burn the hospital and medical school buildings. They concentrated on a small Chinese house at the northeast corner of the hospital compound which was not owned by us, although its roof was continuous with the sheds where our fuel oil was usually stored — most of which Phil had already moved into the hospital cellar. Next to this fuel shed were a number of temporary bamboo shacks which had been used as an isolation ward for cholera patients some weeks earlier.

The gang was determined to fire the Chinese house. If they succeeded, the adjacent structures would catch and pass the flames to the hospital itself and possibly to the entire compound.

Phil seized a heavy pole about fifteen feet long, took up a position in front of the Chinese house, and defied the gang. They argued a long time, the gang insisting the house was Chinese and none of Phil's business, he repeating, "The hospital *is* my business and anyone can see how fire in the small house would gravely endanger the hospital." As their mutual patience evaporated, Phil said that he would brain the first man to put fire to the Chinese house, adding that they would certainly have to kill him before they could get the fire going. He had a very erratic command of Hunanese under the best of circumstances; and in that dramatic scene the unabashed passion and chaos of his language must have created a Shakespearean intensity. The gang consulted among themselves, then told Phil that murder was not part of their mission, and went off.

Frank, James Shen, and the school servants were similarly active across the street on the Yali campus. Frank was told by one member of a fire gang that "the only people who deserve to be called Chinese now are the ones who are giving everything to fight the Japanese — their property, their strength and lives." At one point when a nearby building with cases of ammunition was burning, shells went off in all directions, some whizzing into both the Hsiang Ya and Yali compounds where they mercifully did little damage.

Each of our properties was saved, but the city itself was gutted in the frenzy.

Some dozen hours after the first fires were set Fritz Schoyer took a series of photographs from the Island, showing the lighted waterfront, the large flame footing, and the vast, terrifying cliff of smoke, like the wall of a Grand Canyon in Hell. Safest were the families that lived on junks; most vulnerable were those who were unable to walk out of the city, the invalids, the elderly, and the residents of sections cut off by surrounding fires. We later learned that numbers of refugees who had no family connections near Changsha to whom they could flee had broken into dwellings that had been deserted in the panic of exodus during the first night. Many seemed to have opted to take their chances at remaining inside the city and somehow riding out the fire. A reasonable gamble, but fatally wrong as it turned out.

Behind the fire's facade and to the right in the photograph was Dr. Fritz Eitel's hospital, which was largely destroyed. Before the fire he had added to his regular work the care of several hundred, badly wounded soldiers who slept on straw in a temple across the street from the

233

hospital. About one hundred of these men, unable to fend for themselves at the time of the fire, died in the smoke and flames. The government was reported to have moved some four hundred of their fellow invalids to safety.

When Phil Greene walked through the smoking chaos after heat and fire had diminished, he found pathetic piles of bodies of people who had died in panic-stricken clusters. Down near the South Gate they were so thick in some blocks that he could walk only by hunting for bare spots in order to avoid stepping on corpses, most of them frightfully burned. At the height of the fire, the suffocating lack of oxygen must have been one of the primary hazards. Phil found the city not only charred and flattened, but deserted. He was alone, save for twenty thousand very silent cadavers. A lesser person, or someone without the toughening of medical experience he had had, could easily have gone mad in such a scene of doom and cataclysm.

The repeated explanation of what activated the gangs to fire the city was that the office of the garrison commander for Changsha had mixed up the names of Hsin Chang Ho and Hsin Ho from a telephone message identifying the advance position of the Japanese. The former, a town near Yochou on Tung Ting Lake, was reasonably distant, whereas the latter was a village on Changsha's doorstep. The scorched-earth organization panicked, acted on the basis of the doorstep theory, and rushed into action without orders from either the governor or national headquarters. The Generalissimo arrived in a cold fury on Wednesday, November 16, the third day of the then-diminishing fire. Using the undamaged Hunan Bible Institute for some of his confrontations, he conducted court martials in person, relieved Governor Chang of his regular duties, and saw to the execution on the seventeenth of several of those responsible for the fire — the Chief of Police, for letting his men desert on the twelfth, the garrison commander, and another. The author of the order to burn the city had fled, and we never knew his fate.

· · ·

In the month after the fire, when the missionaries tried to hold together what there was of the city, none was more impressive than Phil Greene. Years earlier in Boston, as a resident at Massachusetts General Hospital when the influenza epidemic had ravaged and demoralized that city, he had greatly admired the performance of an unrenowned doctor who had systematically taken over the work of the devastated staff, done their rounds in addition to his own, made administrative decisions, worked round the clock, eaten his meals, and kept the machinery going until the crisis subsided.

After the Changsha fire of 1938 Phil duplicated that performance. In the panic, only sixty inpatients remained — too ill to walk into the countryside. In line with an earlier agreement, our hospital's Chinese doctors and nurses, during the period of intense danger of Japanese occupation of Changsha, had evacuated the city, leaving at Hsiang Ya only the Americans — Phil and Edna — surgeon and nurse. Phil recruited John Runnalls to assist him first as keeper of the drug room and then in the operating room; Dr. Hsiao Yuan-ting of the regular staff soon returned; Dr. Sheridan from the British gunboat on the river came over to help on rounds, although usually too late and with the internists' toploftiness ("surgery is a craft; medicine, an art"); Winifred Galbraith, a strong-willed and energetic English lady, who taught at the I-fang Girls School, joined them as a nurse's aide; an elderly Chinese lady with bound feet helped, as did Miss Rose Fecker, another member of the missionary community; several servants remained; and Dr. Dmitri Afonski, a White Russian dentist, completed the team. It was as motley a hospital staff as was ever assembled, but they somehow kept Hsiang Ya going, took care of the inpatients, emptied bedpans, produced meals, performed operations, and later even opened an outpatient clinic for about one hundred patients daily, when it became clear that the Japanese were not going to take Changsha at that time and when people had begun to return to the city. It was an epic humanitarian achievement, unreported though it was in the world's press.

To me, Phil's exhausting and heroic work summed up and symbolized the difficulties, shortcomings, and triumphs of medical missionaries in China. For the most part they were shorthanded, did not have adequate supplies or equipment, and may, in their headlong busy-ness, have been behind the best thinking in their field. The medical men and women out in the provinces like Phil, resembled the old-fashioned, American country doctor rather than the gilded specialists of Boston or Chicago. But,

The destruction by fire of downtown Changsha as seen from the Island. (Photo by Preston Schoyer.)

Aftermath of the
Changsha fire.

where the medical missionaries trailed in medical sophistication, they led
in the range and depth of their clinical experience. They had dramatic
and repeated exposure to conditions and diseases that the urban American specialist encountered only as rarities, and that they, the missionaries, handled routinely and with confidence. They were pioneer educators in a particular type of therapy — Western medicine — as well as its
practitioners. The financial rewards were negligible, but the role of the
medical missionary in his region was rewarding in other ways. He was at
once treated with gratitude, exalted as a scholar, and respected for his
devotion.

I found, and still find, the medical missionary at his best to be a
singularly stirring and impressive figure. If the story of the Good Samaritan is as central to the quintessential Christian message as I think it

Aftermath of the Changsha fire.

is, then the medical missionary comes excitingly close to matching role and performance with that Christian ideal.

.   .   .

When I later walked through the residue of the fire's devastation, I saw a flattened city. Changsha houses had no basements; they were neither high nor was the masonry really solid. There had been enough flammables in furniture and furnishings, staircases, wooden beams and roof-trees, wooden doors and window frames, some with paper windows, to create an inferno. When the roof joists had caught fire and given way, the roof tiles dropped; their crashing weight probably explained the elemen-

Next door to our hospital, the arsenal antici-pated the carnage of Changsha when it blew up several weeks before the great fire, smashing all the glass in the hospital and nursing school. John Runnalls was in the hospital stock room at the time, but not injured. He wrote me a few hours afterward about how he rounded up doc-tors and servants to man the ambulance and drove around the corner, where they found about 25 stretcher cases — some very severely cut and burned; perhaps 50 with lesser injuries; and somewhere between 20 and 100 killed, de-pending on how many were buried in the rubble.

tal flatness of the wreckage as much as the follow-up fire gangs. I stood at Pa Ko T'in, the heart of downtown Changsha where the grand silk shops had been, and could see virtually without obstruction for a mile in any direction. One could stand outside the South Gate and see our hospital outside the North Gate. Several weeks after the fire rice was still smoldering where some of the big warehouses had stood. Some shanties had been assembled amidst the ruins, but in general I saw no dogs, no birds, and not many human beings during my walk through the remains of the city.

When Stalingrad was later martyred in the war, its accumulation of nooks and crannies, cellar holes and broken walls, became an intricate, unconquerable redoubt, more defensible than France's Maginot Line. Poor, charred Changsha had no such heroic destiny, at least at that moment in its long history. Burned by fanatics from its own population,

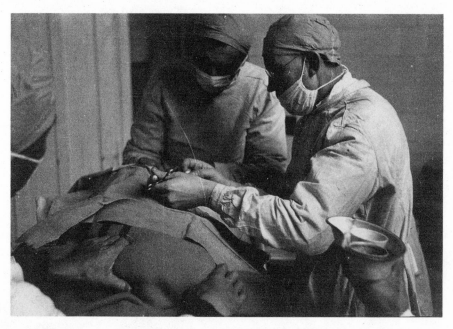

Dr. Phil Greene in operating room, Hsiang Ya Hospital, Changsha; John Runnalls (rear) was drafted as his assistant during the weeks of emergency after the fire.

In those years one saw many makeshift shelters such as this one in Changte, the city of Dr. Tootell's hospital, roughly midway between Changsha and Yuanling.

deserted by all but the missionaries and the sick, it lay flat, wrecked, and totally vulnerable. The Japanese, when they should choose to seize it, would need only take the morning train down from Yochou.

Dr. Biozzi examined my eyes thoroughly and prescribed new glasses which would have to be made up in Hong Kong. That would take time. Meanwhile I was to return to Yuanling, this time in a car that had been hired by Dr. H. C. Chang, the head of Hsiang Ya, and was driven by a chauffeur about my own age with smoldering good looks and a surly manner. Another Dr. Chang (P. S. Chang) of the Chinese Red Cross accompanied us. One of the things that happened to Yali Bachelors over and over again, deriving from our freak status as scholars and Americans, was the opportunity to fraternize with distinguished Chinese. Here was I, a not very exalted Yale B.A., traveling with two august members of

Dr. P. S. Chang of the Chinese Red Cross (on the right). Dr. H. C. Chang (on the left), head of the Hsiang Ya Hospital and the Hunan-Yale Medical College, came from a family identified with Changsha for centuries. One of the first graduates of our medical program, he became professor of internal medicine at Peiping Union Medical College before returning to direct our medical work.

China's medical establishment. H. C. Chang, Hsiang Ya graduate and former professor at Peiping Union Medical College, was from an old and eminent Changsha family. His manner toward me was friendly, interested, and devoid of condescension; we talked about medicine, mutual friends, Chinese poetry, and many other things. The two doctors paid all my bills and lavished politeness on me. In a Changte hotel overnight, scared by the clear night and full moon, ideal for an air raid, I found the usual yin-yang swing of the war pendulum — the delight of the visit with the Doctors Chang and the somber discovery that Changte had been bombed by nine planes between 2:45 and 3:00 p.m. on the same Thursday that my bus for Changsha had belatedly picked me up. Dr. Tootell's sad report was: "1,500 were injured, 200 fatally; 600 had wounds which were dressed at the hospital; 5 died while waiting to be treated; 13 were dead in bed the following morning."

We left early and could see planes dive-bombing near a bridge a couple of minutes in front of us. Probably young pilots practicing. They departed and their inaccuracy allowed us to get through.

War Comes to Yuanling

We know so little about many epic events. For example, when the fires were being set and panic was driving Changsha's population out of the city that first night, where did they go and how did they cope? What happened as they saturated the surrounding countryside? Did friends and relatives in nearby towns and villages really take in any appreciable number? Did families stay together in the traumatic confusion? How many thousands went west into the areas likely to remain outside Japanese control? Going west meant crossing the big, bridgeless Hsiang River. Did the sampan people drive scalpers' bargains—like Changsha's prewar firefighters, who typically negotiated their bill with the owner while his property burned? How many succumbed in the flight; and who buried them?

On my drive to Changte with Dr. Tootell and Mr. Scott I had seen some pathetic figures, ragged and emaciated, who were helping one another westward. They were heart-rending, visible reminders of the Changsha exodus. Dr. Tootell reported that his small hospital had bulged with refugees from the Fire, but how fragmentary our knowledge was—and is—of a great fire which, although unknown to the outside world, actually affected a greater number of people than the more celebrated levelling fires of London, Moscow, Chicago, and San Francisco.

One thing we do know is that the Changsha Fire was yet another situation when public institutions and provisions broke down and when   243 the missionaries played, for the thousandth time, a quasi-governmental role in rallying the forces of succour and repair. A bizarre illustration of this development was when the national authorities decided to distribute emergency funds to Changsha residents and looked around for someone they could trust to get and convey the money to Changsha, it was Frank Hutchins of Yali and Charlie Roberts of the Bible Institute who were asked to drive to Hengyang, receive $400,000 in newly printed $5 bills, and take it to the provincial capital for distribution. They received it, tossed it in the back of the car, and drove back to Changsha as coolly as on a Sunday outing.

Even though Yuanling was moderately distant from Changsha, we had our own contact with the exodus when Mr. Lao helped organize a refugee kitchen on the road between Changte and Yuanling for those who had made it that far. I drove out there with him and, with a number of our students, served the exhausted rows of people who had stopped to eat. For three cents (one half-cent American) someone could get a steaming bowl of vegetables with rice gruel. A person without those three cents would not have been turned away.

For many of our students, the Changsha Fire meant the wiping out of family homes and belongings. Not only that, but without knowing about the safety of their families or whether there would be funds to pay for continued schooling, a great many of these teen-agers were cut off from their parents for the first time. The dean, years later, overwhelmed and embarrassed me with compliments on my having spent so much time talking with the students — unlike the regular Chinese faculty — telling them stories in the evening to keep them occupied and boost their morale. Whatever the dimensions and results of my own efforts, they were gladly given; and the students seemed to me to carry on with remarkable stoicism and even good cheer.

·   ·   ·

Part of the aftermath of the Changsha Fire was that we took more serious precautions in Yuanling for the safety of our personnel. Sooner or later the town would be bombed, not because it had any strategic value, but just because it was there. Our muddy, dingy town was altogether too available, vulnerable, and tempting.

These were the lucky ones—refugees who had survived both the Changsha fire and the two-hundred mile trek into western Hunan.

Two of my most conscientious students helping serve rice and vegetables at the refugee center outside Yuanling. Principal Lao in the background.

I thought that the Senior School, whenever we had a First Alarm, could leave their classrooms and walk onto the ridge which was back of, above, and adjacent to the school property. If planes came, we could throw ourselves into the long trenches that were already there. The latter would have to be cleaned up, since they had been used here and there as latrines, but that could have been taken care of quite readily. However, it was really much sounder to do as the school authorities finally decided — to make what seemed to be over-preparations with a seemingly unnecessarily wide margin of safety. They thoughtfully considered not just safety but interruption, guessing that there would be many more false alarms, occasions when planes would be near enough for a First Alarm, but not close enough to merit an Urgent, or times when we'd get an Urgent but no planes. Given several such episodes per week, the disruption to school work would be massive and demoralizing.

After a good deal of discussion our first step in evolving a safe, simple, and efficient system, was to march the Senior School and faculty up the school steps, out through the back gates, north along the ridge to the large Buddhist temple with its majestic camphorwood trees and their magpies' nests, then down the hillside and east for half a mile into the countryside. All this could be accomplished on a firm, well-worn, dirt path in the time between the First Alarm and the Urgent, particularly since towns, for all their simple technology, quickly developed remarkably effective warning systems. Yuanling was no exception.

Our long file, subdivided by classes, exhibited the students' flair for being orderly and yet relaxed, for finding ways to amuse themselves without flamboyance, gadgets, or games. The weather, clear and cool to begin with, remained sunny, and warmed up. Camera in hand, I went happily about, trying to record that moment of Yali's history, as students and faculty made willing and unselfconscious subjects.

Faculty and students alike had a good sense of occasion, and they extracted evident pleasure from our air-raid practice. The latter was, also, at a deeper level, an opportunity to figure out how we would handle our classes in an emergency. One simplifying factor was that we didn't have to think about the days of bad weather, because planes wouldn't come anyway. The winter of '38–'39 had abundant showers, mist and drizzle, some thunder and intense rain. A perfect washout accompanied the arrival of Chinese New Year, and a downpour a month later came down so fast on our generally well-drained main street that it was over my shoetops. Such weather could be astonishingly welcome. Good weather was, however, a great concern. Moreover, we had to take seriously the rumors that the big Buddhist temple, virtually next door to the Senior School, contained some munitions, probably a very modest cache of them, but worrisome to us. A year later the temple was more obviously military because it temporarily housed the miserable, roped files of army recruits who were marched past the Junior School and through Yuanling toward a yet more wretched destiny at some distant front against well-armed Japanese troops.

Air-raid practice: students and faculty of the Senior School on the ridge just behind our campus. Upturned eaves belong to the Buddhist temple adjacent to Yali and used to some extent for military purposes. Large magpie nest in the tree.

Air-raid practice: senior students streaming down from the gate at the rear of the Buddhist temple; a better route involved walking on the river side of the temple, from left to right, and then coming toward the camera as these students are doing.

Top: Left to right: Dwight Rugh (chaplain), Hwang Chien-hou (assistant to the principal), Mr. Lao (principal), with cane; Mr. Shao (proctor, with arms crossed), Mr. Shen (treasurer, hand on hip).

Dean Ying (center) was lively, principled, unaffected—one of China's top leaders in secondary education. On his right, Mr. Tan An-chi, who taught math and physics.

Mr. Shen (treasurer) and Burton Rogers

Left: He's still not so sure about me.

This boy was one of the veterans of the whole exposure: his genuine smile, telling me that I was forgiven, was for me a moving and ravishing reward.

One way of dealing
with the overpowering sun.

·   ·   ·

Friday, April 21, 1939, was a clear, beautiful morning with a First
Alarm. We got out of the town and onto the top of one of the small hills
to the rear of the Senior School. Those hillsides and hilltops were grassy,
treeless, and usually very bumpy from forgotten graves, but the irregu-
larities of surface offered some protection to a person lying down.

For the first time at Yuanling planes did come. They were close,
perhaps less than a thousand feet up. There were eighteen, divided in
half, with one of the nines going directly over us, the throb of motors
searching our bones. I remember lying face down on that hilltop, dis-
traught with fear, momentarily sure that we were lost. One of my
dominant feelings in those turbulent seconds was the total resentment
that my life should depend on some young fellow up in the sky, my own

252

age but unknown to me, who chose to press the button now or one-half second from now, that interval determining whether I lived or died.

The planes, unknown to us having already unloaded their bombs on a nearby town, dropped propaganda leaflets instead, informing us of the splendors of the Japanese presence in China. Given this unexpected reprieve, I rolled over on my back, relief oozing from every pore, and looked up at the graceful sky as though God Himself were there smiling.

Out of this propaganda raid and our discussions and the air-raid practice, the faculty and administration soon evolved a variant of the rehearsal itself. It involved stopping class work promptly at the First Alarm, walking by class out the front gate, turning right on North Main Street, going the short distance to the far side of the temple, turning right again and walking expeditiously away from the river and the temple for a quarter of a mile or more, to sites where classes could be resumed out-of-doors. I recall a day of wonderful weather in March when the First Alarm broke into my III-2 class and sent us out into the hills where we continued our class discussion of Robin Hood and the passive voice, and where I enlivened even those incongruous proceedings by slipping and falling in the mud. That day had still more to offer, because Fritz Schoyer arrived from Changsha, a wonderful addition to our household and to the English Department.

As air alarms became more frequent, precautions became more systematic, and ultimately a horseshoe-shaped tunnel, with two entrances, was dug into one of the country hillsides. Benches were built along one side, however, only students near the entrance had enough light for study. But school personnel were more apt to be outside anyway.

Despite the interruptions, the inconveniences, and the hazards, teachers and students became expert at dealing with the situation, at making the moves without fuss, and at getting a lot of solid work done.

. . .

Whether veteran or novice, a teacher inevitably has ups and downs. My II-2 class proved to be a group of enthusiasts; they learned a lot, and we got along extremely well. I had my share of successes with III-2, taught just a few classes of IV-2 before someone else took over, and had a borderline failure with V-2.

I remember a particularly vivid dialogue with IV-1 in the second term, when I spent some time describing cast, action, and character in *Hamlet*, unveiling several scenes each day after we had finished our regular classroom work. So much a prisoner of my own love of its cadence and images, I had never really taken in the Mafioso soap opera plot of vindictiveness and accumulating family barbarisms. My students, free of the brainwashing beauty of its diction, saw it more in terms of its essences, its tense scenes and shocking assault upon the family. Hamlet stabbing through the arras into the clamoring Polonius was about the worst for them. Their abundant native skills for theater along with an exposure to the stylized violence of Peiping opera gave them good dramatic insights, and I learned as much as they in the exchanges.

I was often pleased by the willingness of a majority of my students to plough right into the active process of learning to speak a foreign language. It was a grand performance when one considers their transition to alphabet, to different phonetics, to nonreliance on tone, to conjugations, declensions, and related horrors.

The sequels to the cheating-and-hating episode of my Changsha spring were slow in developing. I had somehow coexisted with the ordeal in May and June, stuck with my decision to be consistently friendly and effective as a teacher, and lived it through. During the summer hiatus, when I was preoccupied with travel in West China, my view of the difficulties of that classroom had assumed more reasonable proportions. I was dismayed, however, to find that I was again to have the former II-2, although in their improved Yuanling incarnation as III-1. At this point the class was less than half its earlier size and contained a leaven of new students who might be counted upon as neutrals or possible friends.

I tried my best in the classroom, also visited with them, all this in the school's Yuanling atmosphere of hope and heightened morale. Our relations improved dramatically; we had a hardworking, productive classroom; and the year with them worked out eminently well.

Into 1939

Dwight was the one who made the radio behave, getting the evening news at 8:50 from Manila and at 9:30 from London via Hong Kong. Manila Radio kept urging us to send a box of Tobacolero Cigars to the U.S.A. by Clipper. From the various stations which we could get, we could listen to the points of view on the war of Britain, China, Japan, and the United States. In retrospect, the availability of that diversity seems quite unusual to me. Dwight, by managing the radio contact, kept us in touch with the war's disasters.

In another adjunct to his role as chaplain, Dwight had several interesting encounters with animals. Our neighbors, the Franks, had some ducks and a large gander which wandered loose on one of the terraces below their house. The gander patrolled the area and zealously tried to prevent us from using the walk at one end of his territory. We all became rather nettled over the constant belligerence of lowered neck and outspread wings. I happened to be watching the usual hiss and menace as Dwight came up the stone stairs one day, and saw him lower his own head, spread his arms, and go stoopingly for the gander. The latter fled with the chaplain after him, the goose's clipped wings clawing the air as, with total loss of dignity, he strained for the far end of the terrace. Dwight's nonviolent victory helped markedly in our future relations with the gander.

The other encounter was related to the locating of Burton's bed on the lower veranda, and the accessibility of that spot to two "wonks." Earlier, I had had but little contact with these unloved and unlovely dogs. Happily there were not many of them in the province. Solitary, underfed, and mistreated, "wonks" were slinking curs that appeared to be tolerated around shops as scavengers and watchdogs — and eventual sources of protein (although that wasn't often talked about). In Hunan there seemed to me to be no sense whatever of animals as companions in the American manner. When I gave an evening talk to the Junior School about pets in the States, I had the feeling that the audience and I were on totally different wave lengths — perhaps as Noah would have felt describing floods to a polite audience of alpine villagers.

For some reason, two local "wonks" had become nocturnal, roaming the campus at various times during the night and, among other things, racing onto our veranda and past Burton's bed, all this with much barking. It was maddeningly disruptive, really intolerable. As no ordinary measures kept them out, Dwight took over. It was mid-April when he began taking his gun to bed. After several such nights, I heard him go out soon after the "wonks" began to bark down by the chapel about midnight. Quiet followed, then the blast of the shotgun, the horrible shriek of one dog, and a putting-out-of-misery shot. At 5:30 a.m. another shot roared out, this one from a spot on the veranda right under my bed, waking me with palpitations to hear dog-gasps again.

It was daybreak and one of my III-2 students had just come into our yard "baying" his English lesson. Seeing the dead dog, he sneaked up the hill toward it. Picking up a big stone, he advanced, then retreated, then advanced, followed by excited classmates and the dawning realization that the "wonk" was indeed already dead. When I told the full tale to the III-2 class that day, they roared.

Postscript: Someone (was it the gatekeeper?) retrieved the carcasses, dressed them, and saw that they were eaten.

.   .   .

We had our share of health problems. Burton cracked a porcelain crown on a tiny stone innocently present in a bowl of rice. Such an event was a minor disaster in Yuanling. He used guttapercha as first aid to keep air from the nerve, but really had to undertake the rather complicated trip to

Dwight helping clear
the hillside site for his office.

Changsha for repairs. En route, when approaching Changte by bus, he found that the new autoroad had been deeply and alternately notched from the sides, making it like a slalom course. Further ditching, which could be done relatively quickly, would delay use by the Japanese, then not very distant. When he arrived in Changsha, Dr. Afonsky, the White Russian dentist at Hsiang Ya, fixed the tooth with a new gold crown.

Burton had a much more serious brush with destiny in early December. Some of our Hsiang Ya medical personnel from Changsha had established a small hospital in Yuanling, a mile downriver from the Senior School and on the other side. With some new buildings of unseasoned and unfinished lumber, with their families cheerfully at hand in whatever cramped quarters could be found, with a wooden operating table especially designed by Dr. Liu, and with their surgical instruments only just arrived, our doctors and nurses were ready for action.

Burton chose that moment to be sick for two days. In the evening of the second Dr. Chen Teh was sent for, crossed the river, walked the mile to Yali, examined Burton swiftly and carefully, and diagnosed an acutely inflamed appendix which required immediate action.

We formed a little procession, with me in front swinging a lantern, two of the school servants carrying the patient on a stretcher, and Dr. Chen, Dwight, and Dean Ying in attendance, walked the quiet, dark, deserted Main Street to a clinic at the East Gate where the operation was to take place. Burton signed a release and was given a spinal. While I pumped the pressure lamp Dr. Chen performed a superb appendectomy, and all went well.

I had less dramatic but nagging problems that dragged me down. Pronounced eye discomfort marred most of the winter. There was a long wait for the glasses, my diary reporting bleakly: "Intellectually I stand still, waiting for new eyes." I took to dictating some of my letters to a third-year student.

My glasses arrived via a member of the faculty in mid-February. I wore them with discomfort at first, but with hope that a few weeks' adjustment would give me new life. My first indulgence was to read D. H. Lawrence's *Sons and Lovers*. It was all exhilarating—love's frustration and torture, the mother motif, the great drunken scenes. Lawrence could have written with hands tied behind his back and still seemed a genius to those new eyes.

I had an encounter with sunstroke in the spring, a brief return of zest, and the unlucky development of an acute intestinal disorder. Although no amoebas were found, it was hard for me to believe that I didn't have dysentery. Dr. Liu at Hsiang Ya, short, scruffy, gat-toothed, long-gowned, was right out of the old Mutt and Jeff cartoons, but there was no questioning his medical skills. On the other hand, he dealt with so many major health problems that I felt somewhat embarrassed going to him with merely relentlessly recurrent, watery diarrhea, exhausting though that was for me. In our medical encounters we always laughed a lot, and that may have been the best therapy.

Since the four-mile roundtrip walk to my classes in the Junior School became too much for me, classes were juggled so I could teach just at the Senior School and remain within a safe cruising radius of the facilities. Foreigners in that era, without the benefit of recent alleviating medications, were subject to diarrhea about once every week or ten days throughout the year. So common was it, that one simply lived with it, but mine was much worse, depleting me badly before finally coming under control early in the summer.

.   .   .

Our social life in Yuanling was threadbare by conventional standards. In the absence of movies, radio entertainment, tennis courts, automobiles, pubs, theaters, restaurants, and local tourism, we relied on walking and talking.

On Thanksgiving Day the foreign community assembled at the Frank Buchers' outside the East Gate for stuffed goose and pumpkin pie. The weather was right out of New England — cool with some color in the autumnal foliage.

Another representative act in our social life was when I accompanied Dwight on an April walk over to the Buchers' to chat with Mrs. Bucher, look at her superb Flaming Judas Tree, and meet Dr. Tassis, a newly arrived German doctor who was to serve on the staff of the clinic where Burton had had his operation. Dr. Tassis was one of the sprinkling of Jewish doctors who were being recruited to help out in interior mission hospitals. Escapees from Hitler, refugees who were cruelly fenced out of virtually every country by immigration quotas, these individuals and their families had secured passage to one of the very few places in the world where they were permitted to land and live — the Japanese Concession in Shanghai. Without passports, they were offered entry there and were given shelter, although there were no jobs and no future. To have Dr. Tassis arrive was an event in our social lives as well as a medical advantage. For the hospitals who used these gifted men it was a complication as well as a benefit, because they spoke no Chinese. For the doctors themselves there was the trauma of starting all over again in the boondocks after careers in cities like Vienna, then probably the most advanced medical center in the world.

259

Preston (Fritz) Schoyer came from Pittsburgh, had been educated at Milton and Yale ('33), and had already served a term as Yali Bachelor, 1933–35. An aspiring novelist, he was working on the first of his four novels, *The Foreigners*, which dealt with our lives in Changsha in which, he told me, he wrote me along with himself into his protagonist.

Also in April I walked with Dwight over to the East Gate to call on Maude Russell, a YWCA secretary who was visiting in Yuanling and who talked animatedly about her friendship with Michael Borodin during the period 1924 to 1927 when he served as liaison between the Communists and the Kuomintang in the first of their several periods of cooperation. I was enthralled. That was only a decade earlier and seemed very close to my life. On still another occasion Dwight and I went over to the Hsiang Ya branch to see a member of the Yali staff who was hospitalized. Continuing our walk after leaving the hospital, we passed a broken-open coffin with its grimly exposed occupant partly chewed by "wonks."

We were on our way to supper at Dr. Ch'en's. To eat with the Chens seemed to me a very special experience. They had an unheated, one-room gatehouse for their refugee residence. Here we sat while Mrs. Ch'en, a pretty mother in her early thirties, cheerfully cooked a meal of

Mr. Chang was head of the Yuanling YMCA; Sophie, his wife, was a skilled chemist and a constant visitor at our house.

several dishes, using a charcoal fire in a huo-p'en, a tiny container like a hibachi, on the floor. Expert and unrattled, she saw to it that we were well fed.

After months of our own busy school lives, we had belated but very pleasant spring contact with the Catholic missionaries at the other end of town — Bishop O'Gara, Father Leo, Father Paul, Father Fatty, Father Anthony, Father Nick. They were generous hosts and enjoyed having us come over to listen to the news. On their radio in March 1939, we heard the somber report of Hitler's occupation of Bohemia and Moravia, remnants of the post-Munich, mutilated Czech state. At that point European international politics and indeed world history entered a new and deadlier phase.

.   .   .

A lot of my social life was based on going over to Jeannette Lin's hospital, sitting around her charcoal brazier, and visiting with her and her callers as they came and went. One such afternoon we were joined by Dr. Peng Chi-pu of the Isolation Hospital and Dr. Lo, his wife. Both were 1938 Hsiang Ya graduates, he locally famous as the Yali student who had memorized a geometry book in five days and successfully taken an examination in it.

We went together to visit their hospital, stopping to admire the top beam, the securing of which was being celebrated by wine and paotze (vegetable patties) for the onlookers. We were shown about the new hospital from the bridal suite to the delousing station; there were beds for thirty inpatients — fourteen were already filled with cases of cholera, typhoid, and diphtheria. It was very reassuring to see how the skill and confidence of those two young doctors made the care of highly infectious diseases seem merely routine.

When there were no guests at Jeannette's we usually just sat, talked, kidded and laughed — delightful for me and helpful to her. Despite all her surface gaiety, she worried about being able to maintain her hospital. Moreover, in the event of bombing she was responsible for the safety of her patients, her refugee infants, and staff; and she was uneasy over the renewed uncertainty about whether her hospital would have to move once again, to a yet more remote spot.

"Gondola," Yuanling style. Since her clinic was right next to the river and most of the town was of easy access from the water, Dr. Lin made her medical calls via hospital sampan with this cheerful servant at the oar. She sometimes stopped below the school to see if I could accompany her on these outings.

Her monthly hospital budget, as reported to me for 1940–41, was a masterpiece of frugality: just under $1100 Mex each month for salaries for a staff of twenty-six, from servants to superintendent; medical supplies, $100 Mex; rent, fuel, stationery, and miscellany, $200. Although the monthly total of $1400 Mex in the changing exchange rate figured out to less than $150 U.S. per month, she had a struggle to raise it. The provincial treasurer gave $980 Mex per month, leaving $420 Mex to be made up by income. Since hospital income had never exceeded $350 Mex per month, she feared she would have to cut salaries and even reduce her staff, steps which she hated to consider. Toward the extra expense ($1800 Mex) of building a dugout, she had been given $500 Mex by her superior in the medical hierarchy, but a residue payment remained as well as an earlier debt for the wooden hospital building itself.

She was a marvelous, durable person, loving and thoughtful, a remarkably independent woman in her professional capacity and in the relatively serene way she lived unmarried, a virtual stigmata in China for someone of her age—early thirties—in that era. But she was not indestructible and, as she worried about the hospital, I worried about her. Despite her splendid independence she could have used someone to help with the many aspects of her work that required not only luck for basic survival but talking out and prudent planning.

Although extremely dependent upon each other, we had decided that my plans for graduate work at Yale and her established medical career in China were impossible to fit together, and that we would follow our separate destinies. Neither she nor I could stand the idea of a parting scene. My Yankee reticence and her defensive matter-of-factness meant that what would be splendid in Puccini was beyond our powers of coping and enduring.

One of the bittersweet memories from that spring is of our listening together to the cuckoos that arrived the last of April and were extraordinarily loud, day and night, for two weeks or more, to be succeeded by virtual silence for the rest of the year. To Jeannette the cuckoo said "je je" (big sister), the frenetic repetition unpleasant. To me it had the appeal of a relentless demon drummer who imprisoned his listener between fascination and madness.

Departure

The end of the school year was busy with class photographs that we were invited to join, some festive meals, and the grading of examinations. I was asked to remain for another year but felt compelled to get home and begin graduate study. Yali had confirmed not only my passion for teaching but also the need for systematic preparation for a career of it.

Suddenly my contact with Yali and Jeannette and the whole Yuanling phase of my life was over. Bus passage to Kweiyang became available. I took it and was gone, writing with crumpled heart to Jeannette from somewhere in Kweichow and later exchanging letters that rarely touched our love and admiration for each other.

The bus took me along dirt roads to the west, first through the thread-bare villages and bleak hills of Kweichow, one of the forgotten provinces. I visited our Hsiang Ya and medical school branches in Kweiyang, the provincial capital; called on Joan Wang, friend from Changsha days who was working with the Chinese Red Cross; and saw Shen Yu-ming, formerly of Jeannette's staff in Yuanling and Changsha. Again westward by bus into Yunnan province and the familiar, plateau farmland surrounding Kunming, at the head of the rail line which descended to Indo-China. Beautiful and faded Kunming, not yet the China terminus of the Burma Road, not yet with a disruptive American airbase and overrun with alien soldiers queueing up for women. Its broken wall, grand

Last glimpses of friends on my way out of China:

Above: Dr. Shen Yu-ming, who had now left Jeannette Lin's clinic and moved to Kweiyang to a different medical post.

Right: Joan Wang with the Chinese Red Cross in Kweiyang; formerly of Changsha and tennis-playing fame.

Chang Teh-ch'ang, specialist in economic history; our friendly contacts had begun on the 1937 boat trip between Naples and Hong Kong.

painted gates, and cobblestone streets were my last glimpse of an earlier grandeur in South China. To me this was the city with my favorite pagoda, the one that I was sure both Marco Polo and I had looked upon, he to record the viewing in his *Travels*, I to marvel at its associations.

I looked up Chang Teh-ch'ang, a friend from the 1937 trip by ship to Hong Kong, whose training at the London School of Economics enabled him to teach economic history at one of the Peiping universities taking refuge outside Kunming. One by one the threads were being cut: this was my last contact in South China with a Chinese whom I knew well.

The news from Europe was bad. Hitler had overrun the remnants of Czechoslovakia in March and was now fulminating against Poland, supposedly protected by British and French guarantees. Negotiations for

267

an anti-German treaty of alliance were visibly, but slowly, going on between these two and the Soviet Union. Such a treaty might have reshaped modern history. However, nothing came of it. More effective negotiations which had been quietly started between the Germans and Russians in June were to lead to the flabbergasting Russo-German Non-aggression Pact of August 20, 1939, and the quick invasions of Poland from west and east by both participants.

Although the shape of things was more obscure in July than at the end of August, there was plenty to worry about as I made my way by railway south off the Yunnan plateau into French Indo-China. On the train to Hanoi the explosive news of Wang Ching-wei's defection to the Japanese was published. A famous republican revolutionary, distinguished collaborator with Sun Yat Sen, and archrival of Chiang Kai-shek, he here continued Sun's tradition of making deals with the Japanese, and soon became their figurehead in Nanking in the attempt to give permanency and appeal to the Sino-Japanese Co-prosperity Sphere in Eastern Asia.

I continued to Haiphong, thence by British ship past Hainan Island and along the south coast of China to Hong Kong and Japanese-occupied Shanghai; then homeward by way of Japan. For two weeks I haunted Kyoto, Nara, Tokyo, and Nikko. Kyoto had special meaning for me not only because of my pleasure over its associations with *The Tale of Genji*, but my father had lived there until he was twelve. I visited temples, palaces, and gardens, and watched one of the annual festivals. I was taken to observe a woodblock design being printed, and I bought scores of lovely, inexpensive prints which had been made from newly cut blocks to replace the blocks destroyed in the great earthquake and fire of the 1920s. In Tokyo my friends arranged for me to meet Mr. Mihara, who took me to look at, and buy, yet more prints. He was kind and helpful but never revealed that he was one of the eminent collectors of prints. On a side trip to the elegant Shinto shrine at Nikko, I was particularly moved by the bas-relief panels at the central temple, assuredly among the most beautiful carvings in the world.

All of these unusual experiences were accompanied by the bland insensitivity of my Japanese hosts and acquaintances to Japan's outrageous actions in China — the military blunders and cruelties, the dislocation and compounded tragedies which so vividly filled my mind. As

Last look at the coast of South China.

they seemed totally content with the official clichés about the "China Incident," I didn't know how to react to these new acquaintances — should I thank them for their kindness or tell them what disastrous fools they were to support the government's determination to defeat China in order to avert the threat of communism? It seemed clear enough to me that Japan's severe military pressure on the Chinese government would be the very thing that would most help the Communists by bringing ruin to that government. Japan's policies were soon to prove, in addition, to be profoundly self-destructive. Even by the time of my 1939 visit, her continental expansionism had embedded her deeply in the mainland morass, with no relief in sight, which in turn led to the growing frustration that was to lead to Pearl Harbor, to the vast gamble of South Pacific adventurism, and to the collapse of 1945.

With my own country not yet involved in the war in 1939, my technical neutrality placed me in the unusual position of experiencing one side of the war for two years and now visiting the other side and getting a sense of how little aware the well-behaved homefront was of the barbarism of its army overseas. Caught between kindness and revulsion as I was, and upset over my inability to resolve this dilemma, I was glad enough to move on — by train, Tokyo to Hiroshima and Shimonoseki; by ferry to Korea; by rail on through Korea and southern Manchukuo (then an enormous Japanese puppet-state in the Manchurian northeast of China); and on to Peiping, at that time under Japanese occupation.

My allotted two weeks in that dilapidated old capital contained another visual extravaganza — looking at and photographing the Forbidden City, the street scenes, the wonderful old city walls and great gates, and the Temple of Heaven. The experience, again, was bittersweet. I was lucky to see this remarkable, planned city of the Mongols before so much of it was torn down, rebuilt, and expanded under the Communists. Its faded decadence was very appealing in 1939. There were few prohibited areas, so I could visit the imperial throne rooms of the old Manchu dynasty, the living quarters of the wives, concubines, and eunuchs; the Summer Palace of the turn-of-the-century Empress Dowager; those echoing courtyards, the palace terraces with beautiful white-marble balustrading; and the soft grays and pinks and blues and greens. I felt close both to the bustling agriculture of the North China plain and to the desert. All quite wonderful, and my few American dollars went astonishingly far. But mixed in was a pronounced bitter part — the hated foreign military presence made conspicuous by truckloads of Japanese soldiers being driven about the city's streets. There was beastly summer heat with airless nights, and I caught a severe cold that proved very persistent.

As my time in this former capital slipped away, I was about to embark on a singular rail journey. For a railroad buff, the longest trip by train in that era would have been from South China to Bagdad. I had already gone from the beginning in Kowloon up to Canton and Changsha; also in the winter, on to Wuchang in Central China. Thence the train went north to Peiping (*not* done by me); on up through Manchukuo and across the USSR (about to be done by me); then through Poland to Berlin (not done by me) to pick up the Berlin-to-Bagdad sections (only parts of them done much later).

Thus, when I left Peiping in August 1939, I was embarking on central sections of this wondrously long train ride: in this case, Peiping into Manchukuo, north to Harbin and northwest across the beautiful, gently rolling, Manchurian grasslands to Manchouli, the point of exit onto Russian soil where I was to pick up the connection with the Trans-Siberian Express. The latter, having already come some two thousand miles from Vladivostok, would then take me four thousand miles west to Moscow in a scheduled five days that usually required six.

Part of the drama of this trip was that I was engaged in a race against time. One element was that I had been accepted by the Yale Graduate School, so I needed to be back in the States in time to visit at home with mother and stepfather, catch my breath, and still get to Yale in good shape by late September. But much more important was the basic race against Hitler and the deterioration of the international scene. I needed to slip through Europe without catastrophe or delay. Looking back now at the chronology, one can see what a narrow squeak it was.

Back in Peiping I had known generally that the international scene was deeply troubled by the shrill crisis between Hitler and the Polish government, his chosen target of those August weeks. But no specifics. Nor would there be any for me for over a week, as I was about to join the Trans-Siberian and be cut off from normal news sources.

On the Trans-Siberian, sheltered from harrowing details on German-

Polish relations, I could focus on absorbing the experience that lay at hand. The immensity of Soviet Siberia and Soviet Russia really came home to me as we rattled along, touching base at Irkutsk, Krasnoyarsk, Omsk, and many other exotic spots. Much of the roadbed was so rough that walking down the passenger corridor to the lavatory or diner was an experience in preventing oneself from being thrown to the floor.

I was travelling "hard," the rough equivalent of third class. My compartment had facing seats for eight by day, and for four by night (two lowers and two uppers, each with negligible cushioning). I acquired instant friends among the few foreign passengers. In my own compartment there was a pleasant young Hungarian language teacher who had spent several years teaching French to Chinese in a Catholic school near Peiping. He could manage a certain amount of English, supplemented with French, and we got along famously. There was a lively, hard-mouthed Norwegian who had been a pilot and ship's officer for a line with headquarters in Shanghai. He kidded me about my (nonexistent) sex-life, assuming that I was an aggressive womanizer. I was flattered. He was going home to Norway at a dangerous time. There was a German airline official with a teen-age daughter, en route to Germany. They and the Norwegian lived in the faded splendor of second class.

Our compartment became a modest social center. My Magyar and I were able to have pleasant conversations with some of the Russian passengers who came and went for different stretches. We were often visited by the Norwegian pilot or the German businessman. Together we played *Shanghai Millionaire* (Monopoly). At the station stops, passengers rushed out with containers to get hot water for tea, and we walked up and down for a few minutes, cherishing the exercise and fresh air. Some meals we ate in the diner; some we put together from the food we had been instructed to bring along.

We finally reached Moscow on August 23, a day late but with time for some bits of tourism — Red Square with Lenin's Tomb below the Kremlin wall, walkabout, and wonderful Impressionist paintings in the Museum of Modern Western Art. The big thing, however, was the staggering news of the just-signed Russo-German Nonaggression Pact, which appeared to remove Russian opposition to German aggression against Poland. We were at once assailed with the dominating, openly expressed expectation of a German invasion of Poland. For me, since my planned exit by way of Poland was now fraught with danger and out of the question, this new circumstance created a desperate need to change my Soviet exit visa. I was told that the processing of such an alteration usually required two or three weeks, but the Russian bureaucracy rose to the challenge and changed it within a couple of days. That enabled me to take the train to Leningrad on August 26, do some hasty tourism there, go by train to the Finnish border and on to Helsinki, and catch an early boat thence to Stockholm by August 31, the day before Hitler's invasion of Poland and the beginning of World War II.

What seems in retrospect like exhilarating high adventure was badly compromised by the way I felt. By this time, I was really sick from my dragging Peiping cold and the rundown condition in which I had left Yuanling. Fortunately, a fellow passenger took charge. A New Zealander studying at Oxford, an enthusiastic Marxist visitor to Russia, and a godsend in my condition, she got me into a hotel in Stockholm, where I could collapse briefly in my private race with Hitler. My health now compounded the problem of securing boat passage quickly, before the feared mining of waters would result in the possible cancellation of trans-Atlantic passenger sailings.

I had another bit of luck. A Swedish travel agent from Cook's, fluent in English, kindly came to my sickbed, and without fuss made reservations, fixed up the tickets, and most precious of all got me Atlantic passage for New York. It was up to me now to get out of my sickbed, totter to the station, take the train across southern Sweden to Göteborg, and get onto the *Kungsholm* before its departure on September 3. I managed that, and the *Kungsholm* did the rest. We were shortly through the narrows between Norway and Denmark, as Hitler's mechanized divisions crunched into Poland in the opening horror of World War II.

Epilogue

On August 18, 1939, about two months after my departure from Yuanling, the dreaded raid occurred, a terrible one which leveled much of the town. At Yali, according to Burton, a summer term was being held for students who were stuck there. It had become customary to hold one class early, then have breakfast, and continue promptly with two more classes, the point being to get teaching over before the almost daily interruptions from air alarms.

On this sultry overcast day the Urgent came during lunch very soon after the First Alarm. Twenty-seven planes in three sets of nine flew over and past, swung around, divided into threes, and followed Main Street the length of the town, sowing little black seeds that quickly elongated and then Satanically evoked fountains of debris and towering black columns of smoke. Because the planes kept circling and coming in low for an hour of bombing and strafing, it was seen as a mission for pilots in training. Burton got out and away, going to an area of old grave mounds where he found shelter under a bank. Another wave of four nines appeared and spent another hour or more, leaving behind it a vast black cloud over the town. Burton feared yet another wave, but wanted to get back to the school and into town to help. He met his neighbor Justine Granner and when they heard people shouting above the roar of the fire, they decided to risk a return. Discovering that there had been no bombs on the Senior School, he grabbed a first aid kit and, joined by some 275 students, went along Main Street until fire and debris blocked their way, then turned down an alley to the river steps, encountering clusters of corpses. Finding a surviving baby with a bad head wound, Burton asked who would take the infant through the burning chaos to the hospital. The boy who volunteered was the one suspected by the school authorities of reading Communist literature, a source of worry to them. He went a mile down the beach, barefoot and often over hot rocks, and made it to the clinic.

Somehow the fires got put out, but bomb and fire damage to the town was very extensive. Although many of the Yali students had not gone out of the town at the alarm, none had been injured. Lots of luck there. Subsequent raids were directed at the bus station and the Buddhist temple near the Senior School, but none was as devastating as that first one.

Busy with the complexities of travel across the Soviet Union on my way home that summer, I did not learn about the raid until October, when I was deep in culture shock at graduate school in New Haven. The news, given to me in the midst of the bustling and businesslike Yale-in-China office, made me weep uncontrollably. But I knew well enough that, whatever the dimensions of disasters like that raid, there was always the extraordinary Chinese ability to start life over again, to pick up and get going. Predictably, the school reopened for regular sessions at Yuanling in September 1939 and continued through the war, much in the manner I have described.

In 1941, two years after I had left, the Japanese moved into Changsha. Since that entry took place before Pearl Harbor, American nationals had not yet become Japan's enemies. For that reason Phil, James Shen, and the school servants were able to exploit American ownership of the Yali campus in Changsha as a means of harboring and protecting a large number of Chinese women who were desperately trying to remain out of the hands of Japanese soldiers. Some of those women arrived at the gate having smeared themselves with nightsoil to make their bodies repulsive to the soldiers. Although there were some very tense confrontations, American property under determined leadership could still effectively offer asylum. In that way the campus proved a blessing to many.

After Pearl Harbor the situation altered radically. The Japanese moved onto the Changsha campus, quartered their horses in Frank Hutchins' residence, and built fires on the living room floor. A year later when American war pressures on Japan had become appreciable, the Japanese withdrew from Changsha, burning Yali's chapel, school buildings, and hospital when they left, but sparing the residences. As the war's end approached, with the campus again in Unoccupied China, it was possible for school authorities to begin reconstruction of the campus to prepare for the return from Yuanling of the Middle School, from Kwei-yang of the medical school, and from scattered localities of Hsiang Ya Hospital.

Events were moving too fast—beyond Yali's control. Although the return to Changsha took place in 1946, the attempt at Communist-Kuomintang cooperation at the national level broke down in the following year; the Communists took control of North China in 1948, pushed the Kuomintang south of the Yangtze and then into exile on Taiwan in 1949. The Communists seized Changsha, changed Yali's name to the Hunan Middle School, and initially retained most of the same teachers, but under careful supervision and scrutiny. Later the campus was used as part of a large medical complex, with yet a new name, built up on and around the Hsiang Ya Hospital and medical school. Meanwhile support from the Yale-in-China office was shifted to educational enterprises in Hong Kong, where it remains, supplemented from the 1980s on by the return of Yali Bachelors to Changsha to continue the teaching of English.

It seems to me in retrospect that, by arriving in Changsha in 1937, I was supremely lucky to glimpse Yali's high period, to share in its life and adjustments when the Rape of Nanking traumatized Central China, to observe how the school met the war's challenges with great skill and adaptability, particularly in the removal to Yuanling, and—by leaving when I did, to be spared Yali's demise at the hands of the Communist authorities.

In 1949 an era was indeed over. Missionaries had been at Yali for four decades, had made their contributions, and now were ordered out of the country. Usually one individual in each mission or foreign business was singled out by the Communists for special insult. Dwight was the chosen victim at Yali, everyone else had been evacuated. Placed under increasing restrictions, although never technically under house arrest, he was finally made the butt of a public session in the school gymnasium where his

Chinese friends were expected to testify to his wickedness. He made sure they understood that he expected them to do so for their own safety and the security of their families. Finally, in May 1951, he was allowed to return to the States. Years later he received repeated, embarrassed apologies from one of his former Chinese colleagues who indicated how humiliated he still felt over his own share in the lying denunciations of a man they respected and loved.

The missionary is, by definition, model, witness, sojourner, and withdrawer. His role in China had been abnormally large, and his contributions spread over many fields for a century — off-and-on for much longer than that — it was proper that the job be left in other hands.

In China, with its low life expectancy and relatively few old people, memory is often short, but the residual spirit of the mission is there, absorbed by individuals whom we trained, and incorporated at many points, in the education, science, and medicine of modern China. The residue seems to me vastly greater than the Chinese were allowed to admit during the Maoist generation after 1949.

My era in China was much more puzzling to live through than to view now in retrospect. Although we knew that we were watching the disintegration of Confucian society, no one believed in 1939, least of all Mao Tze-tung, that in ten years the beleaguered Red Army of the poverty pockets of Northwestern China would conquer the country. Our Chinese friends were as baffled as we, as they wandered between two worlds, one dying, the other seemingly powerless to be born.

One of the things Yale-in-China did was to put before the Chinese an enterprise that filled out the weirdly lopsided Chinese perceptions of the West. Years ago Isak Dinesen wrote a brilliant passage in which she pointed out that Western civilization had been presented overseas like "incoherent parts of a mechanism" which the recipients had never seen functioning, and which they could not on their own imagine functioning. More than that, Chinese exposure to the West had been dominated by soldiers and sailors, exploitative businessmen, hard-line evangelists, adventurers, and diplomats. Their actions, their values, and contributions in business and foreign relations were but fragmentary, disassembled, incoherent parts of the mechanism of Western culture. Yali, with its emphasis on the humane values of Western society, on ethical ideals and relationships, served as a corrective which enabled a Chinese, whether Christian or Confucian, more nearly to imagine a functioning Western civilization.

The two years at Yali confirmed my desire to go into teaching, as well as made clear to me that I would be a pacifist when war broke out. I knew no way to get around what I understood as the pacifist witness of Jesus; nor did I know how else to voice my protest over what I took to be the descent toward ultimate self-destruction of the collectivity of independent countries of the world. If each was self-armed and constantly alert to making weaponry more devastating, and if war itself remained periodic and occasionally all-out, did those propositions not strongly imply a foreseeable mutual annihilation? And should not someone, professing to be a Christian, protest against that lethal direction of the state-system? I was unable then, as I am now — as everyone is now — to answer the questions satisfactorily.

For me personally the exposure to China had been exhausting as well as profound. The fatigue, moral, physical, and mental, of the war, with its monumental tragedy, had left me gaunt and depleted. On the way home I was drained by that severe cold contracted in Peiping. I still had intestinal parasites, and for a period there was worry about my having TB. Moreover, I was starved for certain things in my own culture, for museums and symphony orchestras, for movies, ice cream sodas, apple pie and American desserts, and for intellectual conversation on art, literature, and music without an intervening barrier of culture and language. Given such stress and deprivations in China, one would have thought my dominant feelings in returning to New England would have been joy and relief. Yet re-entry created in me an overpowering sense of misery and loss.

At Yale again, this time as a graduate student, part of me felt beleaguered. To me it seemed that no one knew how important China was, had been, and would be; no one realized the depth of my experience; no one understood the fearful dimensions for China — and Japan — of the war's tragedies; no one cared. My distress was enhanced by the drastic culture shock, especially the waste so evident on all sides in American society, made specific before my eyes by the student extravagance at Yale, the fine clothes, the liquor bills, the weekends, the food sent back to the kitchens and thrown out.

It was not unusual for China Hands of the pre-World War II period, whether they had been in business, education, medicine, army, or diplomatic service, to experience a powerful diffuse nostalgia for China when they came back to the West. It was a complex thing. Along with them I had savored China's winning combination of friendship, politeness, and laughter. Even though an alien, often with a camera, I had rarely been exposed to resentment or hostility. As a Yali teacher I had been accorded the revered rank of scholar. My money went quite far. I lived in a well-run household with attentive servants. I shared the togetherness of the school in its exposure to the war. In my environs there was beauty as well as interest and novelty—with an occasional gourmet meal for good measure. Moreover, I enjoyed the expatriate's wicked sense of freedom from the dragging restraint (however loving) of home and neighbors in New England.

Along with these powerful persuaders, these builders of nostalgia, were others—the friends, the personal growth, the challenge, the sense of participation in a pivotal period of history, the insights into circumstances calling for despair but persistently leavened by hope and humor.

All these points, and more, meant that my exposure to China beseechingly haunted me for years.

Central Figures

Hans Borchardt: a German military advisor to Chiang Kai-shek
Minotte Chatfield: Yale '36; Senior Bachelor
Dr. H. C. Chang: head of the Hsiang Ya Hospital
Rocky Chin: recent Yale Ph.D. in international relations; an American visitor
"Gerald": my summer traveling companion in Southwest China in 1938
Phil Greene: member of the permanent staff; chief surgeon of Hsiang Ya
Ruth Greene: wife of Phil; mother of Anne, Ellen, Fritz, and Peggy
Jackson Ho: member of Yali faculty and athletic director
Frank Hutchins: our "boss"; representative of the Yale-in-China home office in
    New Haven
Louise Hutchins: medical intern at Hsiang Ya; wife of Frank
Edna Hutchinson: member of permanent staff; dean of the nursing school
Lao Ch'i-chiang: principal of the Yali Middle School
Dr. Walter Liebenthal: refugee from Nazi Germany; eminent Sanskrit scholar
Jeannette Lin: gynecologist; head of tiny refugee clinic
Burton Rogers: Yale '30; permanent staff; head of English department
Dwight Rugh: Yali chaplain; permanent staff
John Runnalls: Yale '37; my traveling companion to China; Junior Bachelor
Preston Schoyer: "Fritz"; novelist; former Bachelor who returned to help out
Shao Tze-feng: member of Yali faculty; Confucian classicist; proctor
Sid Sweet: Yale '36; Senior Bachelor
Dr. George Tootell: medical missionary at the Presbyterian hospital in Changte
Ying K'ai-shih: dean of the Yali Middle School; one of China's top educators